LOVE BEYOND THE
VATICAN

A Memoir

FRANK J. DeVITO

Printed in the United States of America.

Library of Congress Control Number: 2020919407

ISBN   Paperback   978-1-64803-680-4
                eBook   978-1-64803-681-1

Westwood Books Publishing LLC
11416 SW Aventino Drive
Port Saint Lucie, FL 34987

www.westwoodbookspublishing.com

DEDICATION

I dedicate this book to my children—
Francesco, Leonardo, and Raquel.

They have been my greatest teachers. My children
serve as my personal trinity to inspire me to keep
my heart open and vulnerable, always.

ACKNOWLEDGMENTS

When I first envisioned the process for writing my memoir, I imagined it as it is usually depicted in the popular media: A solitary writer tapping away on a typewriter, smoking a cigarette, and sipping a glass of bourbon. While I admit that I did occasionally enjoy a Dominican cigar and a glass of port as I was typing on my laptop, my vision of what it means to be a writer expanded.

In addition to the solitary aspect to writing, I discovered that a powerful feature of the process is when drafts are reviewed by a diverse group of readers. This is how the text really takes shape and comes alive. Writing, as any art, is essentially a community process.

I want to extend my deepest thanks to my community of reviewers: Cándida DeVito, Chris Kirwan, Cindy Rodríguez, Danielle Queiroz DeVito, Joanna Gallagher, Kathleen Schumm, Marie Culhane, Marina Umaschi Bers, and Terrence Moran. They asked great questions, pushed my thinking, and challenged me to be a better writer.

I had the unexpected experience of having a muse for this book, Elizabeth Imende Cooney. I had my doubts about this project, and Elizabeth would send me late-night texts expressing her love and admiration for my work. What is astounding is that she was reading drafts and providing critical feedback from a hospital room. Her son, John James Imende Cooney, was suffering from an inoperable brain tumor. He died at the age of nine, shortly after I completed the final draft of my memoir. Elizabeth's love and courage inspired me to persist.

The midwife of this book is my editor, Jayne Ogata. I've never given birth, but I think writing a book comes pretty close. Jayne was with me every step of the way. She provided her feedback, revisions, and edits with great insight and compassion. Jayne was relentless in honoring the vision and truth of the text. I am very grateful to her because this project was a "leap of faith." I experienced firsthand that behind every great writer is a great editor.

I would be remiss in not acknowledging the contributions of Jayne's son, Jake Ogata Bernstein. He not only provided copyediting support, but he studied the internal logic and rhythm of the text like a great code programmer and artist. This is a rare gift.

A very special thanks to Westwood Publishing. They took a chance on an unknown writer, and I hope that their faith is rewarded.

I thank you—the reader. There are many other things you could be doing, but you are choosing to read this book. Enjoy.

INTRODUCTION

As you start to walk on the way, the way appears.

~ Rumi

This memoir was a premature birth. I fantasized about writing this book in my retirement, while I was smoking a cigar and sipping a glass of port wine at some seaside apartment. At the time of the writing of this book, COVID-19, a.k.a. the coronavirus, had just begun to disrupt our day-to-day lives. We had no idea what the short- and long-term impact of this crisis would be. You could say that COVID-19 accelerated the writing process. I didn't know whether I would have a retirement in which to write this book or an audience to read it.

This memoir covers a sixteen-year period from 1987 to 2003. In 1987, I was entering my fifth year of seminary training for the Catholic priesthood. I had begun graduate studies in theology at the Pontifical Gregorian University in Rome, Italy, and I was living at the North American College, the residence for seminarians who were preparing to be priests for dioceses in the United States. I was studying to be a Catholic priest for the Archdiocese of Boston.

After much deliberation, I made the difficult decision not to be ordained a priest. In 1991, I became a history teacher at a public high school in Chelsea, Massachusetts, an immigrant city just north of Boston. In many ways, my time there became an opportunity to express another form of priesthood.

Before I wrote this book, I followed an oral tradition of telling my stories at family gatherings and social affairs with friends and colleagues. They were my pilot audience. I enjoyed their reactions— laughter, shock, and sometimes tears. Few people know the details of what happens in a seminary or what the experience of being a high school teacher is like. With a few exceptions, I find media depictions of priests and educators to be unsatisfying. They tend to be two-dimensional and the narratives usually default to portraying them as heroes or villains. From my perspective, the truth is much more complex and compelling.

The arc of my memoir is also a coming-of-age story. Like each of you, I experienced love and heartbreak as I struggled to make sense of my own identity and this thing called love.

I wrestled with my "why" for writing this book for many years. While I had interesting and entertaining stories to share, I was used to sharing them in intimate settings. I wasn't sure how to translate them for a larger, unknown audience. I originally thought that my foot-dragging was just pure laziness or a mañana ("I'll do it tomorrow") mentality. The truth was that I couldn't see my life, and I was wrestling with the deeper meaning of my stories.

It reminded me of a science project I did in high school. I wrote to NASA to send me photos of Jupiter and Saturn that the *Voyager 2* space probe had taken in 1979 and 1981. I prepared slides on my Kodak carousel slide projector—advanced technology in the 1980s—and presented them to my Earth science class.

I thought that the images were miraculous, and I became emotional as I clicked to each slide. My classmates laughed. They didn't understand why I was getting emotional over the solar system.

Why was I getting emotional? I didn't have an answer. Even if I'd had an answer, I wouldn't have known how to explain it.

In retrospect, I realize that I was having a transcendent experience of awe and wonder as I studied the images of Jupiter and Saturn. The primary focus of my science project, for me, wasn't the presentation of information, but the sharing of a transformative experience. The other students clearly didn't share my sense of wonder. I failed to communicate my experience because I didn't have a clear understanding of what I was experiencing.

My heart understood things that my mind didn't fully comprehend.

As I thought about my reasons for writing this book, I realized that before COVID-19, unexpected events had forced me to stop and reassess my life. In 2008, the Boston Celtics won the NBA championship with their "Big Three" of Kevin Garnett, Ray Allen, and Paul Pierce. And I was celebrating my own "Big Three." I became the father of triplets: Francesco, Leonardo, and Raquel. Unfortunately, my celebration turned to anguish because of my children's premature birth. Francesco and Leonardo remained in the neonatal intensive care unit at Brigham and Women's Hospital in Boston for five months. Raquel did not survive and died two days after she was born.

The trauma of my children's birth and Raquel's death led to a dark night of the soul that lasted over a decade. I could feel myself disconnecting from my heart and the people I loved. I struggled to live with a sense of purpose. Life was no longer miraculous but a complicated series of problems that seemed unsolvable.

Writing became my art therapy. Like many artists, I used art to reflect on my personal pain. Writing helped me to find a way through my soul's devastation and heartbreak. Like my science project, I took key scenes and stories from my life and placed them in a metaphorical slide projector. I began to draft my stories. The practice became a personal meditation.

In many ways, it reminded me of the Catholic prayer, the rosary. The rosary began in the thirteenth century and served as the prayer of the people. Because many Christians could not read or had limited access to biblical texts and prayer books, the rosary became a tangible way—using beads—to meditate upon the lives of Jesus and Mary. Like stained glass windows, these biblical stories filtered the light to help Christians to understand the events of their own lives.

I have structured my memoir like a rosary. There are four mysteries: Joyful, Sorrowful, Glorious, and Luminous. And within each mystery, there are five stories, or meditations. Considering the adult content of these stories, some of you may find this approach sacrilegious or offensive. I completely understand. However, I believe that our lives need to become rosaries. We need to dedicate time to reflect upon the events of our lives and allow our hearts to speak to us.

You don't have to be Catholic or religious to appreciate this book. Regardless of your faith tradition, beliefs, or personal philosophies, I hope these stories will resonate with you. Because these stories are about the invitation to love when we least expect it, when we want to resist it, and when we feel shame and regret for betraying it. This memoir is about the daily struggle to be fully divine and fully human. I personally define fully divine as being our true and best selves and fully human as our unpredictable and passionate selves. I believe that the key to happiness is to live an integrated life where we honor the divine and human within ourselves.

I should also say something about the structure of the book. While the arc of my memoir is chronological, the stories and meditations within each mystery are not. I provide timestamps and locations to orient you. You will also notice multiple story threads weave together and apart. You may wonder why I am juxtaposing particular stories, and that is entirely the point—I want you to wonder. It's only through wonder that we can get beneath the surface, to find the sacred in the absurd and the absurd in the sacred. This is the role of the artist. You will never see a paint-by-numbers portrait by Pablo Picasso or hear John Coltrane play a jazz tune without an intricate cascade of notes. I don't pretend to be in their league—yet. But I am walking in the same direction as I create my own path.

I want to give you a heads-up that some strong sexual themes and language are present in this memoir. Their presence is not gratuitous. I chose to be as vulnerable and as real as possible. My family in Honduras are great storytellers and have a sage saying, *"Si vas a abrir la puerta, debes pasar por ella."* "If you're going to open the door, you need to go through it." I am following their advice.

I included a reflection at the conclusion where I respond to readers' questions. Please note that there are spoilers in that section, and my reflection won't be as meaningful if you haven't read the book.

I dedicate this book to my children—Francesco, Leonardo, and Raquel. They have been my greatest teachers. My children serve as my personal trinity to inspire me to keep my heart open and vulnerable, always.

OPENING PRAYER

"Our Love is a Gypsy"

We did not find love in cathedrals
but in the sharing of Rioja wine.
Our love was a gypsy who refused to
follow the maps and guides of dead navigators.
We sometimes lived the illusion
that love had died but breathed a sigh
when we discovered love's perfection.
Our love is perfect.
The world does not recognize
love's perfection.
The world prefers probability to miracles
and dead navigators to gypsies.
Our love is a gypsy and we will dance to infinity
and drink Rioja wine
grown in a vineyard of miracles.

~ Frank DeVito, written for the wedding celebration of a friend

JOYFUL
MYSTERIES

When you do things from your soul,
you feel a river moving in you, a joy.

~ Rumi

GIFT BOX

August 1988 / Rome, Italy

I rummaged through my sparse closet to find a gift box for a necklace. I found a perfectly square box neatly stored on the top shelf. I opened it and stared at the Roman collar for several seconds. I smiled at the irony that the box that housed my dream of being a Roman Catholic priest would become a gift box for my lover, Sophie. I gently removed the Roman collar from the box and placed it on my desk. Then I took the necklace from its brown paper bag and arranged it in the box. The necklace was made from Venetian glass, and the color was an ethereal blue-green that reminded me of Sophie's eyes.

It was the last days of summer, 1988, and I had just turned twenty-four. I was wrestling with the tension between my priestly vocation and my love for Sophie. Having invested five years of my life preparing to be a priest, I had lived with the promise that I would know what I would do with my life tomorrow and the next day and the next. I had found comfort in this certainty. Now I could feel it all falling apart as I thought about Sophie and how much I missed her.

I was living in the Pontifical North American College in Rome, the training ground for future priests serving in the United States. The seminary was located on the via del Gianicolo and was a ten-minute walk from Saint Peter's Basilica at the heart of Vatican City. When I went to the bathroom, I could see the dome of Saint Peter's as I relieved myself in the urinal. It was a surreal feeling to see something that beautiful while responding to nature's call.

I was one of the first seminarians to return to the seminary that late August. Most seminarians were traveling, doing study programs abroad, or visiting with family in the United States. The seminary was big, but it felt gargantuan when I realized that I was alone.

Count Enrico Pietro Galeazzi designed the North American College: a six-story brick and travertine building that sat on twelve acres. The building consisted of a chapel dedicated to the Immaculate Conception, a large dining hall, an auditorium, a library, classrooms, and dormitories. As you walked the campus that was shaped like a hacksaw, you would see a gymnasium, basketball and tennis courts, and a baseball/soccer/football field. The architecture was very Roman, very spartan, and very opulent. A simple walkway with columns and clean lines led to a lavish garden with crawling vines that reached the ornate stained glass windows of the chapel.

I felt an intense anxiety returning to the seminary because its vast emptiness mirrored the expanding fissure that was forming in my heart. I was no longer sure of myself. I was no longer sure of my vocation. But what confused me was that I welcomed the impending earthquake. Beneath the terror of my life collapsing around me, I felt a strange joy.

To re-establish a sense of normalcy, I began to follow the daily practices and rituals that I loved as a priest-in-training. I woke up at 5:00 a.m., showered, and sat in silence for an hour in the seminary chapel. I loved the silence and the solitude. The chapel was dark except for a light that beamed onto the main altar.

I prayed Morning Prayer from the *Liturgy of the Hours*. Also called the Breviary, these are primarily psalms and readings that form the heart of a priest's prayer life. The *Liturgy of the Hours* comes from the Jewish tradition of praying throughout the day and the monastic tradition of reciting prayers at specific hours. The psalms always spoke to me because they were honest and raw. On one particular morning, I prayed this psalm as I was missing Sophie:

Psalm 143: Prayer in Distress

Lord, make haste and answer;
for my spirit fails within me.
Do not hide your face
lest I become like those in the grave.

In the morning let me know your love
for I put my trust in you.
Make me know the way I should walk:
to you I lift up my soul.

In the silence, I was waiting for God. I waited. And I waited. And I waited. No answer. I was hoping that God would light a flare in my heart to give me direction. As I saw the sunlight gently filtering through the stained glass windows, I wondered whether Sophie was that flare.

After morning prayer, I walked to Piazza Navona. I was dressed in street clothes—a grey Boston Red Sox T-shirt and jeans. I only wore my priest clerics to class and to chapel. I decided to go to my favorite cafe that overlooked Piazza Navona. Getting seated was easy at 7:00 a.m., and I ordered a *caffè latte* and a panini with cheese and prosciutto. From my table, I would often gaze at the Fontana dei Quattro Fiumi (Fountain of the Four Rivers), as I did that day. The fountain was designed by Gian Lorenzo Bernini, a brilliant artist of the Baroque period. It was my favorite fountain in Rome because the horse, mythic creatures, and river gods always looked like they were about to leap out of the fountain. I didn't want to miss it when it happened.

As I thought about Sophie, I felt two arms wrap around me, and I heard a voice with a sexy whisper say, *"Padre Frank, dovresti venire al mercato. Le mie pesche sono così succulente e mature."* "Father Frank, you should come by the market. My peaches are so luscious and ripe." Francesca laughed and gave me a kiss. She took a seat across from me. Francesca and her father owned a fruit market at Campo de' Fiori (field of flowers), a rectangular section at the south end of Piazza

Navona. I met Francesca Ricci when I began my theological studies at the Pontifical Gregorian University, attended by seminarians, the religious, and lay people from around the world.

Francesca was a fascinating woman: she audited theology classes but did not believe in God. She was petite with an angular face and choppy dark hair, and she walked with the confidence of a runway model when she entered a room. Her piercing brown eyes always made it look like she was studying you. Francesca was brilliant, and she knew it. She was also a massive flirt. Francesca enjoyed talking about her sex life in front of postulants—candidates who were preparing to be nuns—and would adjust her bra while speaking with seminarians during classroom breaks. When I asked her why an avowed atheist was studying theology, she replied, "I study theology the way that a scientist studies physics. I want to understand how things work from a religious mind. Besides, I enjoy torturing priests and nuns."

As she reached over the table and took a bite of my panini, she said to me, "Please tell me that you had sex this summer. I will be so disappointed if you didn't."

I laughed and replied, "No, no sex, no drugs, and no rock n' roll." I lied about the rock n' roll part—the movie *Dirty Dancing* was very popular in cinemas across Europe.

"There is something very different about you. I can smell it. You can fool those idiot celibates but you can't fool me."

I was a little nervous that Francesca had floated her observation very loudly across the table. She was very proud of her keen analysis.

"I didn't have sex," I replied. This was true. I hadn't had sex with Sophie. I rationalized that I was still honoring my celibate commitment, but I wasn't.

Francesca proudly asserted, "You're a fucking romantic. That's what I hate and love about you. What's her name?"

"Sophie," I replied nervously.

"You are in trouble, my friend. The pope will be very disappointed. This girl has your dick and the pope wants it back." Francesca did have a point in her own crude way. I wondered whether she said things like this to shock the cafe patrons who were sitting nearby or just to shock me.

Francesca asked, "Are you going to leave the seminary? I hope you're not leaving Rome. Now that you've come back to the land of the living, Rome is the perfect place to live."

"I haven't decided," I replied. "I haven't said anything to the rector or my spiritual director."

Francesca got up, slowly sat on my lap, and assured me that I would figure it out. She gave me a kiss on the lips and said, "Look, Padre Frank, being in love is a dangerous thing, and I guarantee that it will fuck you up, but you needed this, my friend. You know where to find me if you ever want to talk."

She hopped off my lap, took a sip of my *caffè latte*, and walked towards her father's fruit market.

Francesca Ricci was a walking Fellini film—she both thrilled and terrified me. When I met Francesca, it was the first time in my young adult life that a woman had taken an interest in me, and I found the attention intoxicating. In high school, I felt that girls never looked at me as a sexual being. If they did, I had no clue. I was the guy that every mother wanted their daughter to date because I was at the top of my class academically, and I was an altar server and volunteer at the local parish church. I had somehow developed an asexual identity that led me to the conclusion that priestly celibacy was probably the right choice for me.

In retrospect, I realized that there were two forces tugging at me. My deep love for the priesthood was a knowing: a knowing that came from the silence, the silence between words. I knew that the world around me was theatre; people were playing roles and felt trapped in their lives. They had stopped listening to the silence, the space that would speak to them about who they really were. I saw priesthood as the cry in the wilderness: the cry to reconnect with the silence, the cry to reconnect with the heart. This force is committed to sacred healing, to radical compassion, and to unconditional love.

The other force is erotic and explosive. Freud coined it the *id*, but it was something much more. This force disrupts plans, ideas, thoughts, and relationships. It can't be controlled and is always seeping through the gaps in life to find expression. Artists have always been able to channel this force. When I was in high school, the TV show *The Incredible Hulk*, with Lou Ferrigno and Bill Bixby, was very popular. I connected with the Hulk. The Hulk and Dr. Bruce Banner represented the duality that I was experiencing in my own life.

During my freshman year in high school, I would do something called "The Hulk." I would arrange for two friends to pretend to beat me up in the back of the class, and I would roll under a desk. As I unbuttoned my shirt, I would start to make animal-like growling sounds. I would then jump to my feet with no shirt and roar at the class as I flexed every muscle in my body. My teachers and classmates loved it, and when the energy was low in class, they would plead with me to "do the Hulk." I had stopped doing the Hulk during my junior year. I was now the asexual leader on campus. My full-time identity was Dr. Bruce Banner.

My struggle was between the priest and the artist, the divine and the human.

I was terrified of Francesca because she threatened my priest identity, and I was drawn to her because she was calling the Hulk. I didn't know her intentions. I knew that she cared about me on some level. Maybe she felt safe with me because I was celibate. Maybe it was an erotic experiment to corrupt a seminarian. But I was certain of two things. First, she was a great friend. And second, I did want to go to the fruit market and try her peaches.

When I left the cafe, it was midmorning, and I decided to attend mass at San Luigi dei Francesi. I loved going to mass at this church because it housed my favorite painting by Michelangelo Merisi da Caravaggio, *The Calling of Saint Matthew*. I was always amazed that you could walk into any chapel or church in Rome and see the powerful artwork of Italian masters like Bernini, Caravaggio, da Vinci, and Raphael.

What I loved most about this particular painting in San Luigi was Jesus' pointing gesture as he was calling the apostle Matthew, a tax collector. His pointing finger, hand, and arm were positioned in the same way as God's in Michelangelo's *Creation of Adam* in the Sistine chapel. It reminded me that the act of creation was not a one-time occurrence but a daily miracle. I wanted to believe that Sophie entering my life was God's way of extending his hand toward me. My life would become a new creation.

After mass, as I was walking back to the North American College, I saw a jewelry store with a window that displayed a stunning blue-green necklace. I felt the necklace was calling me. Imagining Sophie wearing that necklace was better than admiring any artwork in Rome.

I skeptically entered the store, convinced that I would not be able to afford the necklace. A young pregnant woman came over to ask if I needed any help, and I asked about the necklace. She went over to the display case and told me that the necklace was handmade Venetian glass. When I asked about the price, she told me that they were running a special. And when she learned that I was a seminarian, she sold the necklace to me for a very reasonable price.

She asked for a blessing for her and her baby. This happened many times in Rome. Even though I wasn't yet ordained a priest, folks treated me as one. The young mother was apologetic because they had run out of gift boxes. I assured her that it was ok. She carefully packed the necklace in a brown paper bag.

APARTMENT PHONE

June 1988 / Salamanca, Spain

Doña Teresa gently knocked on my bedroom door and told me that dinner was ready. Having recently arrived in Salamanca, Spain, during the summer of 1988, I was still adjusting to eating dinner at 9:00 p.m. My drowsiness was interrupted by the seductive smell of *farinato*, a spicy sausage cooked with pork fat, bread, and onion, and served with fried eggs.

Doña Teresa asked me to say grace before we enjoyed the meal. She and her husband opened their home to university students and visiting professors during the academic year and summer months. At the table were Doña Teresa; her husband, Don Pablo; their teenage son, Diego; and Professor Hugo Carvajal, a visiting professor of Spanish literature from the University of Puerto Rico.

Doña Teresa and Don Pablo spoke to me like I was Jesus. They were devout Catholics, and they had a deep reverence for my presence in their home. This annoyed Professor Hugo. He never called me by my first name—he would simply call me "American."

I angered Professor Hugo the first night when I arrived at the apartment. I had decided to take a shower, and five minutes into the shower, I heard a loud banging on the bathroom door with the bellowed words, "Hey American! This is not the United States where you can use two thousand gallons of water!" Doña Teresa was mortified, and I

heard her yell, *"¡Nunca debería haber permitido un animal en mi casa!"*
"I should have never allowed an animal in my home!"

After I had finished dressing and entered the living room, Doña
Teresa apologized for Professor Hugo and attributed his behavior to
being an atheist. He protested this explanation and said, "What does
being an atheist have to do with American imperialism? He thinks he
owns the world. And what is even more terrifying is that he believes
that his God defends American imperialism." I didn't disagree with
him.

I then shared my views about liberation theology in Latin
America that advocated for social justice, believing that Jesus' vision
countered the inequitable power dynamics within religion and society.
Professor Hugo nodded in approval and said, "Hey American, are you
one of those communist priests? If that's the case, I can tolerate you."

I had gone to study in Salamanca as part of a Spanish language
program sponsored by the University of Rhode Island (URI). Because
the Archdiocese of Boston had a growing Latinx population, I thought
that improving my Spanish would be critical for my priestly service to
immigrant populations.

My mother, Candida Rosa DeVito, had actually connected me
to URI's program. She was also studying in Salamanca as part of her
master's program in Spanish literature at Boston College. My mother
is originally from Honduras and came to the United States as an
immigrant when she was sixteen years old. I admired her courage for
leaving behind what was familiar and embracing a new language and
culture. We were always close. I was glad that we'd be in Salamanca at
the same time that summer because I hadn't seen her for almost a year.

As I was enjoying my after-dinner *café*, I saw the beautiful profile
of a woman walking past the dining room. I wondered who she was
and why she was there.

When we finished dinner, I helped Doña Teresa and her son,
Diego, clear the table. As I was walking down the corridor that
connected the dining room to the kitchen, I saw the woman at the
end of the corridor, sitting at a small table and speaking on a rotary
telephone. When I asked Doña Teresa who the woman was, she

explained that she was one of three students who were renting the apartment on the second floor for the summer.

Doña Teresa explained that the student was using the only phone available for the three apartments.

When I left the kitchen, I noticed that the woman was speaking broken Spanish as she struggled to communicate with the operator. I offered to help her and she said, "I'm trying to reach my father in the United States, but the number doesn't seem to work." As she gave me the phone, she beamed a supernova smile, and I felt everything moving in slow motion. I stumbled with my own Spanish as I spoke to the operator, but I was able to successfully reach her father. When I handed her the phone, she thanked me. As I walked down the corridor toward my bedroom, I felt like I had just survived a lightning bolt blast.

While I was sitting on my bed later, I could hear the bustle of people outside. They were walking to Salamanca's Plaza Mayor (Main Square), where the cafes would soon be filled with international students and vacationers. I began to deliberate about whether or not to join the party. As I was staring out the window, I heard a knock on my door. When I opened the door, the woman was standing there.

"I'm sorry to bother you. I just wanted to thank you for helping me. My parents were worried sick because I hadn't phoned them since I left home," she explained. "My friends and I are heading to the plaza. Would you like to join us? My name is Sophie."

She extended her hand to me, and I slowly took her hand.

"I'd love to," I blurted out before I even thought about it. "My name is Frank."

Sophie was pleased and said, "Frank, could you give me five minutes? I want to change before we head out."

"Sure, take your time," I replied.

When Sophie returned to the apartment, I was reminded again of how beautiful she was. She wore a baby-blue sundress that highlighted the blue-green hue of her penetrating eyes. Sophie Anderson was the girl next door and resembled the actress Elisabeth Shue from the 1980s cult classic *Karate Kid*. She was tall for a woman—five foot nine. Her body was slim, but with the curves of a swimmer; I later learned that she swam for her university's swim team. Sophie had long, dark, wavy hair with bangs and sliced in the middle was a streak of white hair.

I complimented Sophie on her sundress, and she complimented me on my canary-yellow, short-sleeved shirt (she was being polite). I found out that Sophie and her friends were from the University of Massachusetts, Amherst. Sophie was majoring in biochemistry, and her two friends, Marcy and Jenna, hadn't declared their majors yet. They were doing an introductory Spanish program as part of their undergraduate studies. When Sophie discovered that I was doing graduate studies in Spanish, she frowned because she thought that having a mother from Honduras gave me a competitive advantage.

When we arrived at the Plaza Mayor, we had to jockey to get a table. I admired Sophie's tenacity in procuring a table. She verbally spanked a group of intoxicated male college students from the University of Notre Dame when they tried to cut in on a table. When one of the guys tried to flirt with Sophie, she replied, "Look, tell your friends that no one wants to be a part of your Neanderthal frat house. Try your bullshit at a detox center." As I saw Sophie in action, I thought of Professor Hugo. He would be proud that Sophie was fighting against American imperialism. The Notre Dame crew stood down, and we claimed our table.

In the span of a little less than an hour, a polaroid image of Sophie was forming in my heart and mind. She could be sweet, tender, and fierce. I liked what I saw, and I was looking forward to learning more about her.

After enjoying a great bottle of Rioja wine, her friends suggested that we go to a discotheque. Sophie looked at me, trying to discern what I wanted to do. Before I could say that I really didn't feel like going, Sophie told her friends, "Why don't the two of you check it out, and I'll join you tomorrow night."

I smiled at Sophie for graciously giving me a way out.

After her friends left, we ordered another bottle of wine. We began a conversation that I had wanted to postpone for a little while longer.

"Frank, where do you go to school?" Sophie asked.

"I'm studying theology at the Gregorian University in Rome," I replied

"Wow, you live in Rome? That must be amazing. How long will you study there?"

"It's a four-year graduate program. I just finished my first year."

"What happens after that? Are you planning to teach?" she asked.

"I am considering the priesthood."

This wasn't the truth. I had balked at answering her question honestly—*considering the priesthood?* In my mind, I was on an express train to the priesthood—there was no such thing as "considering."

Neither Sophie nor her family were religious. They were Lutheran in name but they weren't active. When I had told Sophie that I was studying for the priesthood, she assumed that I could get married like a Lutheran priest. I was surprised when I discovered that she had little knowledge about the celibacy requirements of the Catholic priesthood. I avoided the conversation about celibacy.

While we were enjoying the last sips of Rioja wine, a *Tuna* (a musical performance group) came to our table and began to sing and play a traditional song from Salamanca. It was a love song that featured a chorus of singers, guitars, tambourines, and a single accordion. As the Tuna played, I studied Sophie as she smiled during their song. She caught me staring at her and reached out for my hand. I felt euphoric as she held my hand.

When the Tuna left, we paid our bill and walked across the Plaza Mayor. As we left the plaza to walk back to the apartment building, she took me by the hand again. She asked whether we could sit on a stone bench that we found along the way. Shortly after we sat down, Sophie hugged me and said, "Thank you for such a beautiful night. I never want it to end." I felt the same. My stomach churned with excitement and terror.

After our embrace, Sophie took my hands and began to caress them. I had never had my hands caressed, and there was something hypnotic about her gentle strokes. I thanked her for doing it. She smiled, and I could see tears forming in her eyes. When I asked her if everything was alright, she kissed me.

99 RED BALLOONS

November 1987 / Rome, Italy

It was Thanksgiving break, and I was excited to take my first trip away from the seminary with some classmates. Our plan was to travel to Florence and Siena in Northern Italy. We left the evening of Thanksgiving Day.

Thanksgiving holiday was strange at the North American College. Most of us were missing our families, and there was a sadness that permeated the seminary.

We did have an incredibly tasty Thanksgiving dinner around 1:00 p.m. The seminary's head chef had added an Italian twist to the traditional dishes. He had marinated the turkeys in garlic, rosemary, and olive oil. The mashed potatoes had parmesan cheese and nutmeg in them. I loved this Italian take, but a number of my classmates missed the traditional approach.

After dinner, we went to the auditorium for a screening of *Ben Hur*. This was a long-standing tradition at the North American College. *Ben Hur* was released during Thanksgiving of 1959, and one of the first screenings of the film had happened at the North American College. The movie producers had given a 35mm copy of the film to the seminary, and we watched the movie on a classic 35mm film projector. I loved *Ben Hur* as a kid, and I grew up watching the film over and over—especially during the Lenten and Easter seasons.

What I didn't anticipate was that my seminary classmates would watch the film like they were watching *The Rocky Horror Picture Show*. There was an avalanche of cheers whenever Ben Hur (Charlton Heston) and Messala (Stephen Boyd) appeared together. Father Stephen Drew, a seminary spiritual director from Indiana, was sitting in front me. He was pretty quiet and reserved throughout the film. When I asked him why so many of my classmates were cheering, he took off his glasses and calmly said, "Frank, I believe it has to do with the homoerotic relationship between Ben Hur and Messala. The guys are celebrating that. You don't see it?" Wow. I didn't see it. I had completely missed it.

The culmination of the viewing happened in a scene when Messala implores Ben Hur to join him because "the future is Rome."

Ben Hur shouts in righteous retaliation, "Rome is an affront to God. Rome is strangling my people and my country and the whole earth, but not forever. I tell you, the day Rome falls, there will be a shout of freedom such as the world has never heard before."

Before Charlton Heston finished his lines, everyone stood up and began to cheer and applaud. I learned that the movie was a cloaked anthem for "sticking it to the man."

In retrospect, I realized that what the Hulk was to me, *Ben Hur* was to my seminary classmates. We felt the oppression of Rome, even if we couldn't articulate it in language. The oppression was not simply about rules and dogmas—this is a simplistic framing that is popular in the media. It was about the inherent contradiction between the stated nature of the priesthood and our human nature.

In the view of the Catholic faith, a priest experiences an "ontological change" (a change in being) when they are ordained. This doesn't mean that priests are better or have a higher status than lay people, but they are transformed into the *persona Christi*, the person of Christ, in order to advance the mission of Jesus to build God's kingdom of love and justice.

I loved this understanding of the priesthood, but it came with inherent problems. In being the *persona Christi*, a priest was not Christ's equal but was sharing in his identity of being fully divine and fully human. The central problem was that there was not a clear theology or understanding about what it meant to be fully human within the Catholic faith. I could also argue that Catholicism doesn't have a clear vision of what it means to be fully divine.

The other challenge was that it set up the appearance of a hierarchy in which a priest has more access to God's grace and power. This is antithetical to the gospels where Jesus presented a vision of the kingdom of God that abolished hierarchy and established a radical equality where we were all the daughters and sons of God. We were all priests. We were all fully divine and fully human.

Some may challenge these assertions, but my seminary experience was clear evidence that we did not have a template or guide to allow for the integration of the divine and human, Bruce Banner and the Hulk, Ben Hur and Messala, the priest and the artist, or whatever you want to call it.

At the North American College, our formation program focused upon four areas:

1. Human: Social-emotional development.
2. Intellectual: Academic training in theology.
3. Pastoral: How to celebrate the sacraments and guide/serve church parishioners.
4. Spiritual: Developing a deep relationship with God.

Each seminarian had a priest who served as a formation advisor who would guide a candidate in the human, intellectual, and pastoral aspects of the program, and we were assigned a spiritual director who was responsible for our spiritual development. We met with our formation and spiritual directors two to four times a month. This framework made sense in theory, but it imploded in practice.

The source of the implosion was the human component of the formation program. From my experience, the other components suffered because the human aspect was addressed at a superficial level. The examples of this are countless but two come to mind. Peter Jenkins, a seminary classmate from Boston, had once locked himself in his room for a week and refused to open his door. I grew very concerned, even wondering if he had died.

I asked one of the priests to open his door, and I saw Peter sitting on his bed. It was obvious that he hadn't eaten or showered for days. When I asked him what happened, he didn't want to talk about it. When I pressed the issue, he yelled at me, "You're a fucking moron. You don't know about me and Dee?"

Dee was the nickname of David Dean, a seminarian from Pittsburgh. They had begun a relationship and they were inseparable. I assumed that they were just close friends, but it was more. Dee had abruptly broken off their relationship. Now it was a case of unrequited love.

When I asked Peter if he had talked to his formation advisor or his spiritual director, he said, "Are you fucking crazy? I would be thrown out of this place in a second. They're only willing to talk about Punch and Judy."

"Punch and Judy" was a term for the type of conversations that happened within formation. They focused on "no punch," or no drinking, and "no Judy," or no women. There wasn't a public acknowledgment that sexual identity was complex and not a monolith. Sexuality was only presented and discussed within the exclusive parameters of heterosexuality. There were pockets of seminarians and priest faculty that would have honest conversations in private.

Unfortunately, the Church had formally advanced that homosexuality was "objectively and intrinsically disordered." This made a number of my seminary classmates feel that there was something fundamentally wrong with them. They may have even entered the seminary as a way to escape their sexual identity. On some level, I entered the seminary for the same reason—thinking that I could avoid grappling with my own sexuality—although the coming months would challenge my delusion that I was, or could be, asexual.

Another case involved a meeting I had with my formation advisor, Father Doug Maguire. When I shared my struggle with celibacy because of Sophie, he replied with a deeply sad expression,

"Frank, you need to leave this place. You're twenty-four years old and you need to be true to yourself. You won't find it here."

I later discovered that Father Maguire had an ongoing relationship with a seminarian from Texas. I remembered when they zipped off in a convertible for a vacation trip to Positano; they had sheer joy on their faces. This was not an isolated incident. There were relationships among seminarians and with priest faculty. From what I witnessed, the majority of staff and seminarians had kept their commitment to celibacy—regardless of their sexual orientation. But there were others, like myself, who struggled to reel in the Hulk.

November 1987 / Florence, Italy

I was at the base of the stairway, waiting to make the trek to the iconic Il Duomo in Florence, Italy, more formally known as the Cathedral of Santa Maria del Fiore. Behind me were my seminarian classmates Jack Donovan, studying for the diocese of Newark, New Jersey; George Foster, studying for the Washington, DC, diocese; and Mike Evans, studying for the diocese of San Diego, California. In front of me were students from the University of Tübingen, in Germany.

As I was climbing the stairs of the Duomo, I noticed the university student in front of me. She was wearing black tights with pink tiger stripes, leg warmers, and a short, black, fitted windbreaker with puffy pink shoulder sleeves. As the stone stairway began to narrow, I had to hunch over to avoid banging my head against the low limestone ceiling. I was getting nervous because I was feeling claustrophobic. The young woman in front of me suddenly stopped, and my face crashed into her derrière. I quickly said, "I'm so sorry." She turned her head around and briefly smiled at me. I was so embarrassed.

I noticed a citrusy perfume scent after my nose had hit her butt, and I wondered if she had placed perfume there or if it was body wash. This speculation helped me with my claustrophobia as we continued climbing. I began to notice how perfectly shaped her behind really was. It wasn't thin. It wasn't large. It was just perfectly round. This became my visual obsession as I climbed the stairs, and it was incredibly erotic.

A part of me wanted to bite her ass. On the other hand, I felt the clear tinge of guilt for entertaining my carnal thoughts. I began to mentally flagellate myself for looking at this university student's ass.

As I was wrestling to contain my inner Hulk, I heard a faint sound of music. I was trying to figure out where it was coming from. When I looked up, I saw that the young woman was now wearing a Walkman headset. I recognized the music: "99 Luftballons" (known in the U.S. as "99 Red Balloons") by Nena. She was listening to the original German version.

This was a wildly popular song in the 1980s. The song was about the release of a large number of balloons in West Berlin and the quick-strike response of the East German military that had sent planes to intercept what they believed was a UFO or a weapon of war. Because of the escalating tensions of the Cold War, something as innocent as balloons could set off a war. This university student's ass was my "99 Red Balloons"—her innocent ass was setting off the conflict within myself.

I was relieved when we finally reached the top of the stairway— we had climbed over a hundred steps. I was inspired by the view of Florence from the top of the Duomo. It was late afternoon and the entire landscape had a terracotta hue that made everything shine.

As I was admiring the view, Jack Donovan came up to me and said, in his thick Jersey accent, "So how far did you stick your nose up that German girl's ass?"

I pretended not to know what he was talking about.

"Come on, Frankie, I saw it. It's ok. Just don't get any ideas."

Jack had become my best friend in Rome. He was honest, real, and a fiercely loyal friend.

While I was at the top of the dome, I looked for the German girl. I saw her, and she noticed that I was staring at her. She smiled at me. I heard bubble gum snap in her mouth, and she blew a large pink bubble. This girl really liked pink. Her university friends pulled on her jacket to get her to leave, and she said to me with a giggle, "Goodbye, Captain Kirk."

As they were descending the stairway, George came up to me and asked, "What was that all about?"

George Foster was a sociologist and had taught at American University in Washington, DC. He had entered the seminary at age thirty-six. Most seminarians at the North American College were in their early to mid-twenties. I loved George because he had a gift for saying the craziest thing possible during the course of a conversation. During our first religious retreat in Assisi, Italy (the home of Saint Francis), one of the seminary spiritual directors was giving a talk on the spirituality of the priesthood.

When he opened it up for discussion, George said to the group, "Father, with all due respect, I find the priesthood of the New Testament to be completely sterile in its customs and rituals. It's boring, and I mean boooring.

In the Old Testament, we had priests splashing blood of sacrificed animals on altars. They lit up mounds of incense. It was a pure spectacle that really inspired the faith and devotion of the Jewish people. Now all we have is a few drops of holy water that we sprinkle on babies during baptisms. Our sacraments no longer have any real power."

Our retreat house roared with laughter after George spoke. In one statement, George had completely misrepresented two major world religions. Some of the seminary faculty and students disliked George because they thought he was pretentious and pedantic. I loved him because he was always coming from left field with his comments and insights.

As we descended the staircase from the top of the Duomo, I was thinking about the young German woman. When we arrived at the bottom, we exited the church and decided to walk around the Piazza del Duomo. I looked around to find the young German woman, and she was eating a *gelato* with her friends. I began walking towards her, and Jack shouted out to me, "Hey Frank! Where are you going? Oh God. Are you still trying to meet the German girl? Didn't you get enough of her ass?" I pretended not to hear Jack, and I continued walking toward the young woman.

Suddenly, I felt something stab me in the back. I turned around and faced a man—about sixtyish—who was small in stature, with white hair and a trimmed beard. He was wearing a tweed jacket that had small tears at the shoulders and cuffs.

"Pardon me," he said in a British accent. "I didn't mean to startle you. I am a bit lost." I saw that he was holding an umbrella and realized that he had poked me with it. He continued, "And I am hoping you can help me to find my way home." The man said that his name was Sebastian and explained that he lived in the area, but he had become disoriented.

When Jack, George, and Mike caught up with us, Jack was annoyed with me and said, "Can you please stop thinking with your dick and let go of the German girl?"

When Sebastian heard Jack's comment, he said to me in a fatherly tone, "Son, I should warn you that German women tend to get fat when they get older. You should listen to your friend."

Jack looked at me quizzically and asked who this man was. Sebastian told my friends what he had told me. Jack pulled me aside and whispered, "You are fucking unbelievable. Is your goal to meet every single fucking stranger in Florence?"

Jack turned to Sebastian and said, "Look, we're just touring Florence. We don't know this city."

Sebastian nodded and replied, "My apologies for bothering you."

I could see that Jack was beginning to feel sorry for the stranger, and he said, "OK, we'll do what we can to help you."

Sebastian was very happy with the offer for help and replied, "Boys, I want to buy you a meal."

We started walking toward a trattoria that Mike had found in his guidebook. George was not happy. In a low voice he said to us, "How do we know that this guy isn't a serial killer? The DC police used to work with me all the time to develop profiles for killers. This guy fits the profile of a killer."

I burst out laughing and Sebastian wanted to know what I found so funny. I lied and told him that I was laughing at his comment about German women becoming fat. He nodded and replied, "They really do."

When we sat down at the table of the trattoria, we looked at each other as we studied the menu. I kept looking at the small rips on Sebastian's jacket. I didn't want to embarrass Sebastian and order anything that he couldn't afford. Sebastian assumed that we were struggling to understand the menu and said, "No worries gentlemen. I speak fluent Italian. Let me do the order."

I enjoyed hearing Sebastian speak Italian with a British accent as he ordered for the entire table. For the first plate, he ordered a round of *insalata di pomodoro* (tomato salad). He also ordered a bottle of white wine.

While we were eating the salad, he excused himself and said that he needed to use the restroom. Immediately after Sebastian left the table, Jack amped up his Jersey sarcasm and said, "I will bet you a hundred dollars that he skips out on us."

George responded, "I don't care about the bill. This guy is a murderer. We need to leave right now. Did you ever notice in horror films that the protagonists never leave when they have the opportunity?"

Mike, who had been pretty quiet through most of the trip, said, "I don't think he has any intention of scamming us, and he is sure as hell not a murderer."

Mike grew up in San Diego and worked as a truck driver before he entered the seminary. He was street-smart and grounded. I enjoyed being around him because he was unassuming and had a dry sense of humor. During our comedic adventures, Mike was happy to play the straight man.

When Sebastian returned to the table, he clapped his hands and said, "Gentlemen, I have good news. I remembered who I am and where I live. We need to celebrate." He proceeded to order *carbonara* (pasta with egg, cheese, and cured pork), *bistecca fiorentina* (grilled steak), and *gelato alla nocciola* (hazelnut ice cream).

While we were eating the gelato, a woman came to our table and gave a big hug to Sebastian. It was his daughter, Grace. Sebastian thanked us, and he left the restaurant accompanied by his daughter. Jack began to laugh and said, "I knew it. The guy just skipped out on us." When we called the waiter for the bill, he told us that the English gentleman had already paid it.

As I savored the gelato, I thought about how much I needed Sebastian in that moment. His kindness was helping me to salvage the last remnants of my innocence. The German woman who heralded my personal "99 Red Balloons" reminded me that it was slipping away.

JOYFUL MYSTERY 4

CONVENT COURTYARD

August 1988 / Seville, Spain

I kissed Sophie in the courtyard of a convent in Seville, Spain. The convent was constructed in the thirteenth century and was a striking example of the Mudéjar architecture that reflected the intertwined histories of Islam and Christianity in the region. I kissed her under a cluster of fruit and palm trees that protected the intimacy of our moment. I couldn't stop kissing Sophie—it felt as special as when I first kissed her on a stone bench in Salamanca.

After we kissed, I noticed that Sophie had tears in her eyes. This was the second time she had cried since we had first kissed. I asked her if everything was alright.

"It is," Sophie replied. "It's just hard for me to explain."

"Just try," I encouraged her.

"I love you, Frank." This was the first time Sophie had ever vocalized these words. My heart knew she loved me, but it was still a surprise to hear it.

"I love you, too," I replied. I felt some shame because I hadn't had the courage to tell her first. We had only been together for seven weeks. I thought she would think I was a freak.

After I told Sophie that I loved her, she smiled and then looked down. Sophie began to rain tears.

"I'm sorry," she said, then explained: "I'm afraid. I'm just afraid."

"Afraid of what?" I asked.

"At some point, this is all going to end. That's why I cried when we first kissed and why I'm bawling now."

"Why does it need to end?" I asked. As the summer had progressed, I had avoided all talk about the seminary and my celibacy commitment. I wasn't sure if she assumed that I would end the relationship when I returned to the seminary. In my heart, I had placed my priestly vocation in some kind of limbo. I was happy to live in the present, and I tried my best to avoid all thoughts about the future. My priority was to assure Sophie that we had a future.

Sophie replied, "Everything dies. Everything just dies. When I was a kid, I was always studying shellfish, birds, insects, animals, whatever I could get. I asked my mom why everything died, and she told me that nature works in a cycle. We're on a hamster wheel of life and death. When I started studying biochemistry in the lab, I could see this at the molecular level. Things just die."

"I understand things die, but don't we have some time to enjoy?" I asked. "Are you saying that our relationship has the shelf life of a fly?"

I realized that Sophie wasn't specifically referring to my seminary commitment as the reason for why our relationship might end. She was sharing her personal truth about the fragility of relationships.

Sophie began to laugh and said, "A fly will die in about twenty-eight days. We've at least made it to seven weeks."

July 1988 / Salamanca, Spain

After we met in late June of 1988, Sophie and I became inseparable. The summer language programs in Salamanca were six weeks long, and we made sure to wring every moment we had together. Our days had an Eden-like rhythm that I loved. We would walk together to the University of Salamanca after breakfast, where classes ran from 8:30 a.m. to 12:30 p.m.

Each day I visited Sophie's classroom during my morning break and did something absurd outside the window of the classroom door to make her laugh. I did my best Charlie Chaplin schtick: pretending to go down an elevator, or holding a bunch of tree branches while I imitated an explorer.

After class, Sophie and I had a daily ritual of going to a market and buying some bread, cheese, and fruit. We would sit on a park bench and enjoy our lunch. Around 3:00 p.m., we'd go to swim at a public pool that was popular with international students. Sophie enjoyed kicking my ass whenever we had swimming races. Afterwards, we would sunbathe and read out loud to each other. Sophie loved mystery novels and we read *The Name of the Rose* together. She thought I would enjoy a murder mystery that happened in a monastery.

At 5:00 p.m., we'd go to a local library to do our homework. Then we'd walk over to the plaza around 7:00 p.m. and enjoy a coffee or beer. And at 9:00 p.m., we'd return to Doña Teresa's apartment for dinner.

I had fallen out of grace with Doña Teresa because she thought I was violating my priestly vows. Even though I had not yet taken vows, I understood her sentiments. Professor Hugo loved it. He was no longer the sole object of Doña Teresa's scorn. He also liked Sophie and said to me, "Hey American, I understand why you like that American girl. She has a natural beauty that you don't find in a bottle." Hugo continued, "She's smart because she's studying to be a scientist. That American girl will make a good atheist. She will definitely keep you on your toes."

After dinner, we'd meet up with classmates and friends in Plaza Mayor, enjoy drinks, and listen to Tunas. We typically stayed in the plaza until 3:00 a.m. We'd then kiss and talk on our stone bench and return to Doña Teresa's around 4:00 a.m. It took me a good hour to unwind, and I'd fall asleep around 5:00 a.m.

I would wake up at 7:00 a.m. and do it all over again. I was astounded that I could survive on two hours of sleep per night. But I was too happy to be tired.

During our six weeks together, I had stopped discussing the seminary with Sophie. Somehow my love for Sophie was like bubble-wrap around my anxiety about what I would do once the summer was over. The only time I became anxious were the moments before I went to bed and the first moments when I got up. As soon as I saw Sophie, my fears would evaporate like the morning dew.

The only time that Sophie and I fought was the day that I did a Superman flying performance outside her classroom window. I wore a light blue, long-sleeve shirt and a red windbreaker. I wrapped the arms of the windbreaker around my neck to make it look like a cape. I imitated Superman by making a flying motion with my arms and having my classmate shake my red windbreaker behind me. In Christopher Reeve fashion, I turned to the window and smiled as I waved. The classroom broke into laughter and began to applaud.

To my chagrin, the teacher opened the door. I thought she would reprimand me, but she invited me into her classroom. She was a young teacher from Madrid named Lucía, and she said, *"A nuestra clase le gustaría conocer al bromista que nos ha estado entreteniendo durante varias semanas."* "Our class would like to get to know the prankster who has been entertaining us for several weeks."

Lucía invited me for drinks later in the evening. When I met with Sophie in the library to finish our homework, I told her that her teacher had asked to meet with me. She frowned and asked why. I told her that I didn't know. Sophie asked me to swing by her apartment after I met with Lucía.

I met with Lucía in a cafe in Plaza Mayor. I didn't realize how beautiful she was until I saw her outside the classroom. She was medium height with a very curvy build and shoulder length, chestnut colored hair that was pulled back in a ponytail. Lucía wore black, fitted capri pants and red flats. I tried not to stare at her breasts peeping out of the plunging neckline of her crimson red blouse. When Lucía gave me a hug, I noticed she smelled like soapy lavender.

We ordered beer, and I waited for her to explain why we were meeting. She gave me the choice to speak in Spanish or English. After I flubbed with my Spanish, she began to speak in English. I was impressed with her fluency. She had grown up in Madrid and had recently completed her graduate studies in education at the University of Florida. Lucía was closer to my age than Sophie was. She was twenty-five and I was twenty-four; Sophie was twenty-one and had just finished her junior year of undergraduate studies at UMass Amherst.

Lucía wasn't forthcoming about why she had wanted to meet with me, and I finally asked her. She took a sip of her beer and told me that she was flattered with the attention I was giving her. I was completely confused and asked her what she was talking about. Lucía explained, "I was trying to make it easier for you. You did a different trick every day outside the door of my classroom, and I was wondering when you were finally going to ask me out."

I didn't know what to say to her. I had been a nerd my entire life. For the first time, I felt as if women were taking notice of me. And I loved the attention. It was completely intoxicating. It felt good— really good. I knew that I loved Sophie, but I was physically and intellectually attracted to Lucía. My stomach churned with anxiety and excitement. I rationalized my attraction to Lucía by believing that I could bathe in her attention as long as I wasn't compromising my emotional connection to Sophie.

Lucía looked at me intently, waiting for an answer. I finally replied, "I'm incredibly shy. I've always been shy around women."

Lucía began to laugh and said, "Your performances are a very public act and yet you are shy? I've heard that many actors are introverts."

She was right. I was an actor. I did feel guilt for misleading Lucía and for potentially compromising my relationship with Sophie. My decision to mislead Lucía was intentional and misguided. I had neither corrected her assumption that my daily performance was for her, nor did I tell that I was performing for Sophie, my girlfriend. I let her believe what she wanted to believe, absurdly thinking that I could maintain my innocence.

We had dinner together and talked through the night.

Lucía was a fascinating woman. She had an acute intellect and a dark humor that I enjoyed. The conversation was different from the daily interactions that I had with Sophie. Lucía was well-versed in world affairs and social justice causes—topics that were close to my heart. My conversations with Sophie tended to focus upon our experiences in Salamanca: the events happening in our classes, the pool, the plaza, the food, the drinks, and Doña Teresa's apartment. Our love was deeply connected to everything that was Salamanca.

I heard the bell of the clock tower in the Plaza Mayor strike 2:00 a.m. I was so absorbed in my conversation with Lucía that I had lost all sense of time. I began to panic when I realized that I was supposed to meet up with Sophie. I stood up abruptly and went over to Lucía to give her a quick hug. While I was thanking her for a great night, she pulled me in close for a kiss, but my lips did a quick detour to her left cheek. I could see the disappointment in her eyes, but I didn't explain my abrupt departure and lukewarm kiss.

I ran to Doña Teresa's apartment building and bounded up the stairs to Sophie's apartment. I softly knocked on her door and then began to knock harder. She didn't answer.

Sophie did not meet with me the next morning. She had left for class without me. I didn't go to perform outside her classroom door, because I was afraid to face Lucía. When I looked for Sophie after class, I didn't find her. I was finally able to catch up with her in the library.

Sophie wouldn't look at me. She simply asked, "Did you fuck her?"

"You know I didn't," I answered in an offended tone.

Sophie angrily replied, "How would I know that? I've known you for a little more than a month. I was wondering when you would get bored."

I understood why she was angry, and I knew she was right. But defending myself became the higher and misguided priority. "Look, she's your teacher. She invited me. What was I supposed to do—say 'no'?"

Sophie quickly retorted, "You spent the whole fucking night with her."

I pleaded, "Look Sophie, you're right. I was supposed to meet up with you, but I lost track of time. I'm sorry—I don't know what else to say."

I didn't do my homework that night. I spent the next two hours assuring Sophie that she was the only woman of my heart. I was trying to calm her down like a hostage negotiator. Sophie finally relented, and we went to the Plaza Mayor for drinks.

August 1988 / Seville, Spain

As we sat in the courtyard of the convent, I thought of Sophie's insight that everything dies. Our six-week summer program had come to an end, and we had decided to spend the next two weeks traveling through southern Spain before Sophie returned to the states and I returned to Rome.

We were traveling with my mother and with Anne, a graduate student from the University of Rhode Island who had become good friends with my mother. Our plan was to make our way to Málaga, the birthplace of Pablo Picasso, before we returned to Madrid for our flight home. We were staying in the convent in Seville because my father had sponsored the education of a young Honduran nun, Sister Irma, who was now serving in the convent in Seville.

I knew that my mother had been quietly observing my relationship with Sophie. During the course of the summer, my mom had never shared her views about it with me. She was smiling and gracious whenever Sophie was around, but I could see a nervousness in her demeanor.

I intuitively knew that my mother didn't think that Sophie was the right woman for me. She had never expressed this to me, but I felt it was true. My mother preferred quiet and reserved women that she perceived to be modest. I thought this based on my experiences during family trips to Honduras when I was in high school. Whenever young Honduran women had shown an interest in me, she would always recommend the quiet women who had reputations for being modest. This preference might have been cultural.

Sophie was neither quiet nor reserved. She could be brash, and my mother observed this whenever we were sightseeing or enjoying a meal at a cafe.

While I was sitting in the convent courtyard with Sophie, I heard a loud bang. The noise spooked us, and we looked around to see what it was. Then we heard another loud bang, and another, and another. When I looked up, I saw that the nuns were abruptly closing the wooden shutters of the convent windows that faced the courtyard. The chorus of banging grew louder. The nuns were upset that we were in the courtyard. And they weren't subtle. They had probably seen our hugging and kissing, and they were expressing their displeasure.

The next morning when we went to the 7:00 a.m. mass, I approached the pew where my mother and Sister Irma were sitting. Sophie and Anne came to the chapel together, but Sophie was not allowed to sit next to me. Sister Irma instructed her to sit in the pew that was three benches behind us. Sophie began to quietly laugh, and she was shushed by a nun standing next to her.

My amusement that the nuns were trying to separate us was short-lived. Sister Irma flashed me a disappointed look as I tried to suppress my laughter over the nun's intervention. My mother leaned over and told me that several of the nuns had witnessed the kissing that occurred in the courtyard. The symphony of slamming shutters we had heard the previous night was phase one of their plan to salvage my priestly vocation. Phase two was separating us during mass. After mass, as we entered the refectory where we ate, I saw phase three in action—Sophie was assigned to eat with the novices (nuns-in-training), and I was to sit with Sister Irma and the Abbess (the head of the convent).

Sophie kept looking over at me and smiling—she was amused by the organized separation. I wasn't as amused. I had known Sister Irma as a child, and she had been ecstatic when I made the decision to enter the seminary. When I arrived at the convent, Sister Irma had shared with me that she prayed daily for my vocation. I hated disappointing her, but a part of me knew that I was entering a new phase in my life, and I had no idea where it would lead.

FRIGID MIRACLES

March 1989 / Lourdes, France

Marcel asked me to assist a pilgrim who was in a dressing room, preparing to enter the bath. A striped blue and white cloth shower curtain covered the entrance to the room. I called into the dressing room and asked if I could help. A man replied in a husky voice, "*Estoy teniendo problemas con la sábana. ¿Podrías ayudarme a ponérmela?*" "I'm having problems with the sheet. Could you help me to put it on?" When I entered the dressing room, I saw a tall, pale middle-aged man who weighed over three hundred pounds. The single sheet was not enough to cover his frame, and I tied two white sheets together to cover him. He had a mummified look when I finished tying the sheets around him from his torso to his feet. His name was Diego and he had come from Barcelona, Spain, for the healing baths of Our Lady of Lourdes.

Jack Donovan and I had traveled to the sanctuary of Our Lady of Lourdes, in France, to serve as volunteers for two weeks. We worked for the Hospitalité Notre Dame de Lourdes (Our Lady of Lourdes Hospitality), a Catholic confraternity that was responsible for assisting pilgrims who traveled to the sanctuary.

Our Lady of Lourdes was the title given to Mary, the mother of Jesus, who had appeared to Bernadette Soubirous, a young adolescent girl who lived in extreme poverty. In 1858, Bernadette experienced a series of visions of Mary, and in one of these visions, she was directed to clean herself at a nearby grotto that flowed with muddy waters. The next day, the waters of the grotto flowed clear, and Bernadette told local townsfolk that "the Lady" had instructed her to build a chapel above the grotto.

News of these Marian visions spread very quickly, and people began to make pilgrimages to the site. Many of them shared their personal miracle stories of experiencing a healing of mind, soul, and body when they drank or touched the spring waters. A church and sanctuary were constructed, the crutches of healed pilgrims were suspended from the ceiling of the sanctuary, and photos were posted on the walls.

Making a pilgrimage to Lourdes was the Catholic version of attending the Super Bowl or the World Cup. Jack and I had anticipated that volunteering at Lourdes would feel like we were actually playing on the field. We were excited to be a part of it. The baths were the most popular destination for pilgrims who wanted to experience the healing springs of Lourdes.

When I escorted Diego to the bath, he had problems walking because I had wrapped the sheets so tightly. We entered a small, spartan room that had walls of grey brickstone and a rectangular tub made of smooth stone that was partially sunken below floor level. The only items on the walls were towel hangers with blue towels and a small white statue of Mary attached above the head of the tub. I warned Diego that the water was frigid and told him that we would do our best to make him comfortable. The real miracle of the baths at our Lady of Lourdes was that people did not die from hypothermia.

Jack was on one side of the tub and I was on the other as Diego stepped into the water. The policy was to pray in the language of the pilgrim. In the case of Diego, we prayed the Our Father, Hail Mary, and Glory Be in Spanish.

Typically, a pilgrim would bend down and splash some water on their face, or they would slowly sit in the tub and submerge their head and body. Instead, without warning, Diego did a reverse swan dive. Jack and I tried to catch him because we didn't want him to smash his head on the stone tub. We were completely unsuccessful, but fortunately Diego's head had narrowly missed the edge of the tub. Jack and I fell to the floor as waves of spring water leapt from the tub and drenched the two of us. Diego immediately jumped up and cried, *"¡Gracias Mary! ¡Gracias Jesús! ¡Estoy curado! ¡Puedo sentirlo!"* "Thank you Mary! Thank you Jesus! I am healed! I can feel it!"

Diego was so ecstatic about his healing that he didn't notice the sheets had slid off his body. He was completely naked as he did a boxing motion with his fists. He began to jump up and down in the tub, crying *"¡Le gané al diablo! ¡Lo noqueé!"* "I beat the devil! I knocked him out!"

I looked over at Jack, and he was rolling on the floor in a convulsion of laughter. I slipped again on the floor as I was scrambling to grab towels to cover Diego's naked mountain of a body. As I laid on the floor laughing, Diego alternated splashing water onto me and Jack. Marcel, the French volunteer coordinator, ran into the bath and began to yell, *"Pour l'amour de Dieu, que se passe-t-il?"* "For the love of God, what is going on?" Diego then began to splash water onto Marcel.

Every evening, the volunteers had a meeting to debrief the day and to outline the plan and assignments for the following day. Every volunteer coordinator provided a brief report about the activities of their team. When it was time for Marcel to report, he said, "The team did some good work today. We were able to overcome some logistical challenges in supporting pilgrims to successfully access the baths." Then he looked at me while saying, "I am concerned, however, that some members of our team are not taking their responsibilities seriously. They are taking a circus approach to serving people at the baths." Jack then playfully elbowed me and said, "Yeah Frank, get with the program."

Behind his back, Jack and I referred to Marcel as "Mr. Hospitalité." We thought it was ironic that a team coordinator for hospitality would have such a zealous commitment to being inhospitable. Marcel was only twenty-seven years old. He was small in stature—five foot three—and had a prominent widow's peak under thick black hair that he slicked back. He reminded me of Dracula, and like Dracula, he sucked the life out of any room he entered.

Marcel was a Catholic zealot. When we first arrived, we were required to attend an orientation meeting. Marcel took the opportunity to share his personal beliefs about the core tenets of what it meant to be a "true Catholic." Marcel looked suspiciously upon me and Jack because we were Americans. From his perspective, American Catholics practiced a deeply flawed and diluted form of Catholicism. He was deeply concerned about the view of some American Catholics that women should be ordained. Marcel attributed this position to the feminist movement in the United States. The sexual revolution of the 1960s and 1970s, in Marcel's mind, was the advent of sexual promiscuity among Catholics in the United States.

He was even more concerned when he found out that we were studying to be priests. He feared we would be complicit in spreading modern Catholicism, which in his mind was antithetical to the true mission of the Church.

When I peeled away his words, I realized that he had a deep nostalgia for a Catholicism that he had never actually experienced. He lived his own brand of "Make Catholicism Great Again." It was a brand of Catholicism that excluded people and uncoupled Catholicism from its social justice roots, which emphasize inclusion and human rights.

Fortunately, Marcel was an aberration among the volunteers and leadership of the Hospitalité Notre Dame de Lourdes. Most team members exuded a warmth and joy that gave pilgrims hope as they waited to enter the sanctuary. I was particularly impressed with the care and attention that they gave to pilgrims with disabilities. They made them feel at home, and pilgrims experienced being a part of a larger human family.

After Diego had playfully splashed Marcel with spring water, Marcel glared at me and ran out of the room.

When I was finally able to retrieve towels for Diego, I covered him and he stepped out of the bath. He gave me a bear hug and then a kiss on the cheek, and he thanked me for assisting him with his miracle. I learned from Diego that he had lost both parents to cancer and had fallen into a deep depression for three years. Diego explained that no amount of therapy or drugs had worked, but now he felt the lightness and joy of a child. I was very moved by his witness, and I escorted him back to the dressing room. When he learned that I was a seminarian, he asked, "Father, please pray for me. I want to live the rest of my life with the joy of a child. I didn't think this was possible until now."

Diego reminded me why I wanted to be a priest. There was always something powerful about facilitating and being witness to the *shift*—conversion and healing. It wasn't the water that brought the shift; the water was an instrument, but not the source. The shift was a perfect act of grace during which someone made the courageous decision to no longer live in their pain. Our suffering and pain sometimes serve as dysfunctional friends. They define us and limit our beliefs about who we are and who we could become. Through his faith, Diego healed himself. In the gospels, Jesus reminded folks that their faith was the source of their healing (Mark 5:34). I never saw Diego again, but I wanted to believe that he was still experiencing the world as a child—in all its beauty, wonder, and mystery.

March 1989 / Lourdes, France

When we had first arrived at Lourdes, the housing coordinator for volunteers had no record of our reservation. I did not speak French, and Jack did his best with his high school French. Jack told him the name of the person who had taken his reservation over the phone, shaking his head in disbelief as he listened to the housing coordinator's reply. He turned to me and said, "If I'm hearing him right, the guy who took down our reservation has died! God forbid that we would actually have a normal trip."

There was no room in the main hostel for us, so they opened the hostel annex. The annex looked like a hospital psychiatric ward from the 1920s. It was a large open room with white walls and dormitories that were separated by shower curtains. Since we were the only two people staying in the annex, they did not provide us with heat or hot water. When Jack went to take a shower, I heard him yell, "My fucking brain is freezing. If the water temperature drops one degree, I'll be taking a shower in a fucking hail storm."

We affectionately referred to the hostel annex as "Cellblock 13" because of a song I made up about it. Most nights I was shivering as I struggled to sleep. One night, as a way to help me forget that I had lost all feeling in my toes, I began to sing a bluesy melody that echoed off the institutional walls:

Cellblock 13

Cellblock 13, cellblock 13.
Be careful of what you dream in cellblock 13.
I ain't telling you no lie, that I want to die.
Cellblock 13, cellblock 13.
Be careful of what you dream in cellblock 13.
Flies are falling from the sky and landing in my eyes.
Cellblock 13, cellblock 13.
Be careful of what you dream in cellblock 13.

Eventually, Jack would join me in the chorus, and this song became our nightly ritual before we fell asleep.

When we made our daily trek to Lourdes, we always looked forward to connecting with one particular volunteer, Arthur Robinson. Arthur was a stately, middle-aged British gentleman, and we looked forward to the days when we were assigned to work with him. In the spectrum of humanity, Marcel was on one end, and Arthur was on the complete opposite end. Arthur was gracious, compassionate, and exuded a radiant joy. Jack and I used to imitate him when he prayed the Our Father in a melodic British accent that sounded like the actor Anthony Hopkins.

Shortly after we met Arthur, he shared his story with us. Arthur was raised Catholic, but during his university years he had become an agnostic. The turning point in his life was when his eleven-year-old daughter, Olivia, was dying from leukemia. She was in stage IV, with little chance for survival. Olivia asked her father to bring her to Lourdes when she saw the movie *The Song of Bernadette* on TV and learned about the healing spring at Lourdes. Arthur reluctantly brought her, believing that offering her false hope was incredibly cruel. After Olivia visited Lourdes, however, the leukemia went into remission and never returned.

Arthur returned to the Catholic Church and began to attend daily mass. He finished his story with this final thought: "When Olivia was healed, I realized that I had experienced an even greater healing. Olivia suffered from cancer of the body, but I suffered from a cancer of the soul. I went from believing that life was just a random series of probabilities to believing in the daily synchronicities of miracles. I experienced my own personal 'Big Bang.' My heart exploded in a million directions and formed galaxies and universes of faith, hope, and love."

SORROWFUL MYSTERIES

Sorrow prepares you for joy. It violently sweeps everything out of your house, so that new joy can find space to enter. It shakes the yellow leaves from the bough of your heart, so that fresh, green leaves can grow in their place. It pulls up the rotten roots, so that new roots hidden beneath have room to grow. Whatever sorrow shakes from your heart, far better things will take their place.

~ Rumi

SORROWFUL MYSTERY 1

FATHER ANDREW

April 1988 / Rome, Italy

In the early morning of April nineteenth, I heard a quiet knock on the door. I wasn't sure who would knock on my door this early in the morning. I ignored the knocking, assuming that I had imagined it. I heard a second quiet knock. I jumped out of my bed and opened the door. Paulo, the telephone operator for the seminary, told me that I had an important call. I walked to a small phone booth located on the third floor of the seminary. When I picked up the receiver, I heard my mom's voice on the line:

"Francis, we lost Papa last night. I'm sorry, honey."

"Oh no..." I whispered. "What happened?"

"Honey, he collapsed in the parking lot when he arrived for work. The doctors couldn't revive him," my mother explained. "Will you be able to come home for the funeral?"

My world collapsed into the surrealism of a Salvador Dalí painting. The phone didn't look real when I stared at the receiver. I looked around the small phone booth, and I felt the walls closing in on me. I told my mother that I would be at the funeral and I hung up the phone. My father had died on "Patriots' Day," a local state holiday commemorating the first battles of the Revolutionary War, and it also marked the annual Boston Marathon.

A couple of weeks earlier, the seminary and the Christian world had celebrated Easter Sunday. I was now living Good Friday with no hope for an Easter Sunday.

It was a little before 5:00 a.m. when I had spoken to my mom, and I spent the next two hours wandering through the streets of Rome. I saw Italian workers setting up barricades in Saint Peter's Square as they prepared for the daily throng of tourists. Water was running through the square as workers pressure washed the cobblestones. I walked to the church of San Luigi dei Francesi, hoping that it would be open. The door of the church was propped open, and I saw an old man washing the large green, red, and white stone tiles. I went to Contarelli Chapel and knelt on the worn wooden kneeler. I was there for one reason. I needed to see Caravaggio's *The Calling of Saint Matthew*.

I studied the image of Jesus, hand extended and finger pointed. In the painting, Matthew's face is illuminated by a light. But the light breaking into the darkness of the room is not coming from a window—or from Jesus. The source of the light is unknown. It simply shines on Matthew, who sits there pointing to himself, wondering if he is the one being called.

While I stared at the painting, I wanted to cry, but I couldn't. I felt completely detached from my physical body. I walked back to the seminary at 7:00 a.m. to prepare for morning prayer. As I entered the main foyer of the seminary, Joey Richards, a bubbly seminarian from South Carolina, greeted me with an enthusiastic, *"Buon giorno Francesco! Tutto bene?"* In a subdued voice, I replied, *"No, niente è buono."* "No, nothing is good." Joey put his hand on my shoulder, and I shared my news with him.

He immediately took me to the "red room," a community lounge with a large red door where seminary faculty and visiting clergy socialized. The red room was off limits to seminarians, but Joey pushed open the door and scampered to Monsignor Timothy Walker, the rector of the North American College. Joey explained the situation, and Monsignor Walker extended his hand to me in condolence. He assured me that his secretary would arrange a ticket for my immediate flight home. Monsignor Walker kept his promise: later that morning, I was on a flight home to Boston.

My father, Francesco Rafael DeVito, was known as Father Andrew. He had been a Catholic missionary priest in Honduras for the Order of Friars Minor, known as the Franciscans. They were founded by Saint Francis, and they wore chocolate-colored habits with a hood and rope cincture. While he was serving as a priest in Honduras, he met my mother, Candida Rosa Méndez, in a remote municipality of northern Honduras called Las Limas. My favorite photo of my parents was of my father, wearing his Franciscan habit, standing next to my mother under the umbrella of an *aguacate* tree.

When I told my father that I had decided to enter the seminary to become a Catholic priest, his reaction was a combination of pride and concern. He still had a deep love for the priesthood, but he also knew the social stigma of leaving. My father and mother were demonized by their families and the larger Catholic community when they made the decision to be together. They received over two thousand pieces of hate mail that threatened them with hell and damnation. He didn't want me to experience this.

I assured my father that becoming a priest was what I really wanted. He knew that I was an unusual kid, and I felt out of place within my peer groups. I was reading the theological works of Augustine of Hippo and Thomas Aquinas while my peers were partying to the music of Madonna and Journey. I made the decision to enter the seminary during my senior year in high school. When my guidance counselor asked me about my "back-up school," I told her that I was only applying to the seminary. She thought this was crazy and called my parents. My father answered the phone and in response to her concerns he said, "Frank is his own man, and I am with him till the end of line. If he wanted to join the circus, I would support him 100 percent."

My decision to enter the seminary was deeply affected by my father's Catholic faith. He exposed me to both the beauty of Catholic spirituality and the realities of institutional dysfunction within the Catholic Church. Even at an early age, I was able to distinguish the two.

I was raised on stories of Saint Francis, and my father was still close to some of his seminary classmates who served as priests and brothers in the Franciscan Order. I enjoyed spending time with them because they had a childlike exuberance that was so different from the other adults in my life. My teachers and the parents of my friends looked beaten down by life. Life was a fight and they were losing.

Two of my father's friends, in particular, had a powerful connection with my family. Brother Joseph, who had served as a missionary with my father in Honduras, weighed almost four hundred pounds, and he fit the description of Friar Tuck from the books and movies about Robin Hood. Having served as a cook in the seminary, Brother Joseph always brought a large suitcase full of food when he visited: assorted deli meats, cheese, jams, bread, chocolates, and cookies. Before Willie Wonka, there was Brother Joseph.

My father's other friend was Brother Anthony, who always had a car trunk full of sports equipment. He would bring us to the local parks in Stoneham to play pick-up baseball, basketball, and football. The neighborhood kids loved Brother Anthony because he was a kid himself. He didn't ignore them like the other adults in their lives.

While I enjoyed Catholic spirituality and the company of Franciscan Friars, my father was very transparent about the dysfunction of the institutional Church. He shared personal stories about how leadership within the Church had undermined the work he was doing in Honduras. In addition to attending to people's spiritual needs, my father had worked within the villages of Honduras to finance the education and training of youth so that they could earn a living wage, and helped to build roads so that local farmers could deliver their goods to the larger cities within Honduras. When the leadership within the Church discovered what my father was doing, he was reprimanded and told that he was a priest and not a social worker. My father believed that the heart of Catholic spirituality was in the social mission of the Church: that is, following Jesus' command to feed the hungry, clothe the naked, and visit the prisoner.

My father was also an avid historian, and he shared with me the tragic chapters of the Church's history: the Inquisition, forced conversions, slavery, and the mass genocide of Native peoples as Catholicism spread into the Americas. Despite these horrific events, he never felt that the Church's crimes and misdemeanors eclipsed everything that was good and beautiful about the Catholic faith. I have always been deeply grateful for this distinction.

I have often wondered how my father's choice to be a priest affected my decision to enter the seminary. I believe that it did have a profound impact that any therapist would find couch worthy.

My father never told me this, but I could feel it: he carried a burden. He felt a deep guilt for leaving the priesthood. While being married and having children was a choice he never regretted, he struggled to reconcile that with his decision to leave the priesthood. On some level, I felt guilty for being born. While legally my birth was legitimate, I was illegitimate, morally, in the eyes of the institutional Church. Becoming a priest would not only serve as a vindication of my father, but a vindication of my very existence.

That said, I have never considered my decision to become a priest as a psychological compulsion. I made an authentic choice to enter the seminary, rooted in the profound belief that the priesthood was aligned with my identity. If I did have access to a time machine— knowing what I know now—I would choose it again.

My father was born to Italian immigrants in the North End of Boston, MA, the Little Italy section of the city. When he left the priesthood in the early 1960s, he had to work odd jobs like cleaning toilets; no one would hire him for professional jobs due to the social stigma of having left the priesthood.

He decided to take the postal exam and successfully became a postman. It was a difficult work schedule; he worked evenings and nights. I would see him at 3:00 p.m. before he left for work, but I didn't see him most mornings because he went to bed at 4:00 a.m. Regardless, I always thought that being a postman was a perfect job for my father because of his love for geography and history. A work colleague and friend, who frequently visited the house, shared stories of my father figuring out the obscure addresses they came across when they were sorting mail.

What I loved most about the man formerly known as Father Andrew was his humility. He had two uniforms that he would wear for work, and two sets of shirts and pants that he would wear outside of work. He was never into accumulating things or doing things for social status. My father drove an old Chevy station wagon with rust forming on the white roof and royal-blue body. One day, a school friend who visited my house regularly noticed that my father wore the same shirt every day—a short sleeved faded denim shirt with small rips. I felt some embarrassment after my friend shared this observation with me. I reluctantly told my father that I was embarrassed by the way he dressed, but he wasn't upset. He calmly said to me:

> Francis, the world will always measure you. That's the reality of life. You will never have enough money. You will never have enough clothes. You will never have enough cars. Your house will never be big enough. You will never be successful enough at your job. Remember the words of Thomas à Kempis ['The Imitation of Christ'], '*O quam cito transit gloria mundi*.' 'Oh how quickly the glory of the world passes away.' Francis, don't focus on the things that don't matter. Focus on the things that matter—the things that last. It makes all the difference in the world.

Though as a kid I felt embarrassed that he wore the same shirt every day, after he died, "*cito transit gloria mundi*" reverberated in my heart. I felt shame for the times I had been ashamed of him. I regretted not writing to him more often. I regretted not calling him more often. The beautiful truth was that none of this mattered to him. He lived with the knowledge that he was proud to be my father and that I was proud to be his son.

When I returned to the seminary in May of 1988, I saw a pile of letters and cards on my desk. Most of them were from classmates and seminary faculty expressing their friendship, love, and sympathy.

I laughed when I opened up a small package from Francesca. It was a box of condoms with a note that read, "*Devi scopare quante più donne possibile. Ti amo. L'amore sempre, Francesca.*" "You need to fuck as many women as possible. I love you. Love always, Francesca."

As I read through the cards and letters on my desk, I had one letter in my backpack that I hadn't yet read. I wasn't ready to read it, but I decided to open the envelope anyway. It was a letter from my father that my mother had given me when I arrived home. It was found in his coat pocket by one of his coworkers. The letter was dated April 18, the day that he died. My mother explained that she typically had to coax my father to write letters to me. On this particular day, he took the initiative to write me on his own:

> *Querido hijo* (Dear son),
>
> *I'm trying to get this letter out to you today before I head off to work. Your mother is laughing at me. I don't know why, but I don't know what I would do without her. I enjoyed the photos you sent of you and your compadres in Florence and Greece. You looked like a very happy crew. It must have been wonderful to walk the streets of Da Vinci, Giotto, and Michaelangelo. Remember that their blood is in you. You always have the power to create something beautiful.*
>
> *I received your postcard from Assisi—the birthplace of Saint Francis. Remember that you are a son of Saint Francis. You were named after him. Always follow the way of simplicity. Don't get caught up in the ways of the world.*
>
> *I have to go now. Your mother is calling me. Be well my chum. Keep the faith!*
>
> *With love, your father,*
> *Frank*

It was very easy for me to hear my father's voice as I read the letter. He was relentless in warning me about the "ways of the world." It was always connected to "*cito transit gloria mundi.*" There were many points in my life when I didn't follow his advice. I gave importance to things that were not important. I lost sight of the things that were truly important.

I slouched in my chair as I thought about him.

As I sorted through the letters and cards on my desk, I found a letter from the University of Rhode Island, welcoming me to their summer program in Salamanca, Spain.

SORROWFUL MYSTERY 2

BAMBINO GESÙ

October 1988 / Rome, Italy

I heard a loud cry outside my window and a woman shout, *"Mio Dio, mio Dio! Questo è un incubo. Come potrebbe Dio fare questo a un bambino innocente?"* "My God, my God! This is a nightmare. How could God do this to an innocent child?"

I lived on the third floor of the seminary, and it faced a children's hospital called Bambino Gesù (Baby Jesus). Through the large window in my room, I could see the balconies of hospital rooms. After the shouting, I heard deep sighs and sobbing, and I saw a young couple embracing each other on one of the balconies. Then the young woman broke the embrace and engaged in a frenzy of shouts and piercing screams. The young man tried to calm her down, but she remained fiercely inconsolable.

I pulled my desk chair up to the window and I sat there, staring into the night. It was about 2:30 a.m. The young couple had left the balcony and returned to their room. I was thinking of the woman's question, "How could God do this to an innocent child?" I was wondering what it would be like to be a parent and to be vulnerable to this type of heartbreak. On some level, I felt the young woman's rage, and I found myself praying for her. My prayer was more of a demand than a request that God do something.

The hospital wing of the seminary that faced Bambino Gesù was a unique community. Most seminarians preferred not to live in the hospital wing. They preferred the spaces that overlooked Saint Peter's Basilica and the neighboring churches, the courtyard, the athletic field, the gardens; they preferred any space to the hospital wing.

Each seminary wing had a priest who served as a kind of resident assistant, or RA. Our RA was Father Stephen Drew from Indiana. He was a spiritual director and also served as the business manager for the seminary. When I first met him, I liked him because he looked like a younger version of my father. He was average height (five foot six), with a round face and dark brown hair peppered with gray. Like my father, he wore the FBI-style eyeglass frames from the 1960s. He wasn't particularly warm, but he was always accessible and observant. The door to Father Drew's room was always open, and seminarians would regularly congregate there to laugh or to cry.

Creating a warm and inclusive culture was a high priority in the hospital wing. Two seminarians served as the leaders in building this culture: Sean Williams and Patrick Spencer. Sean was from Alabama and spoke with a clipped Southern drawl. There was not a day that Sean did not check in on me and offer support or assistance. He was always impeccably dressed, and he took pride in wearing his priest clerics when he went to class and to chapel. He was average height with an athletic build, and he walked with a purpose. Whenever a seminarian was ill and couldn't attend chapel or class, Sean was diligent in bringing meals to the seminarian's room. No matter the day, Sean was upbeat and ready to *carpe diem*—seize the day. From my perspective, he embodied the best of us, and he loved living on the hospital wing.

Sean had heard the tears and cries from the young woman on the balcony. He asked me, "Frank, did you hear the commotion last night? My heart just broke for that poor girl. I wanted to cry with her." He meant it.

"Yeah, I heard it," I replied.

Sean gave me a big hug and said, "Thanks for noticing it. It's hard to watch, but we need to notice. They're the people of God. Those are the people we serve."

Sean said things like this all the time. At times, I found it annoying. In this case, he couldn't be more right.

Patrick Spencer was the other culture builder of the seminary's hospital wing. He was tall, blond and blue-eyed, and his chiseled profile reminded me of Captain America. Patrick was from Pittsburgh, PA, and he came from generations of family members who served in the military. He walked like a soldier and talked in short choppy sentences.

Unlike Sean, Patrick didn't exude warmth and friendliness, but he made you feel that he would take a bullet for you. He held us accountable but never in a punitive way. There was one day when I had skipped out on class with Francesca, and we went to her father's market for some cheese and fruit.

While I was walking back to the seminary, he came up behind me and asked, "How was class?" He smiled, wrapped his arm around me and said, "There are a lot of people counting on you to be great. Allow yourself to be great."

What does it mean to "allow yourself to be great"? At the time, I dismissed it as empty advice from an upperclassman who wanted to keep a younger seminarian in tow. If anyone else had said this, I would have rolled my eyes to the back of my head. Because Patrick was so sincere and authentic, I heard him.

Years later, I still hear him. I've wrestled with this question since Captain America first challenged me over thirty years ago. Over the years, I've come to a more integrated understanding of greatness: allowing ourselves to be fully divine—our best and true selves; and fully human—our unpredictable and passionate selves. The world needs Dr. Bruce Banner *and* the Hulk. While the seminary was a flawed institution, I believe that it did help me in a profound way on my journey to become fully divine and fully human.

August 1987 / Rome, Italy

As the airplane circled Fiumicino International Airport to prepare its descent, I felt excited as I saw a shining sea of terracotta roofs. I straightened up in my seat to drink in the view, thinking that I was the luckiest guy in the world to have the opportunity to live and study in Rome.

While I was pondering the miracle that was Rome, I heard sniffling from the person seated in front of me. I knew he was a seminarian because twenty-five of us had met at John F. Kennedy Airport in New York City to take the direct flight to Rome, and I thought I remembered that he was from Newark, New Jersey. I kicked the back of his seat and asked him why he was crying.

He turned around and blurted, "It's none of your fucking business. But if you need to know, I'm thinking about my family. I miss them already." He extended his hand and told me that his name was Jack Donovan.

"Jack, I'm a little confused—you're leaving Newark to go to Rome and you're crying? Is there something about Newark that I don't know?"

After I said this, I introduced myself and we began to playfully banter.

Jack replied, "It figures you're from Boston—you're all pricks. If I were you, I would be excited to leave that shithole. Boston is a mecca for assholes."

I didn't disagree with him and we began to laugh.

When our plane landed, I headed to the baggage claim with Jack, and we were still verbally jostling with each other. Two seminarians dressed in clerics greeted us: Sean Williams and Patrick Spencer. They helped us with our bags and told us that they were assigned to serve as our mentors.

October 1988 / Rome, Italy

I had only slept a couple of hours—I was still haunted by the piercing screams of the young mother on the balcony of Bambino Gesù. As the morning light peeped into my room, I saw that the young mother and her husband were no longer on the balcony. I wondered whether God had answered her prayer—and my prayer.

The great thing about seminary living was that it was very structured, and I didn't have time to feel sorry for the young mother. While some seminarians felt that it was overly structured, I never felt this way. I enjoyed the rhythm of the day.

We had the following schedule:

7:00 a.m. / Morning Prayer
We gathered in Immaculate Conception Chapel and prayed the *Liturgy of the Hours*, a compilation of psalms, hymns, biblical readings, and prayers. We sometimes went old school and sang Latin chants and traditional organ hymns. Other times we had folk groups lead us in Catholic folk songs that sounded like John Denver music. I had no complaints about the music because I love John Denver.

I was part of a folk group called "The Preach Boys." We would take Beach Boys songs and playfully bend the lyrics for a Catholic twist. For example, the Beach Boys classic "California Girls" became "Roman Catholic Girls." And we sang the lyrics:

> The Eastern Rite girls are hip
> I really dig those styles they wear
> And the Baptist girls with the way they talk
> They knock me out when I'm down there.

> The midwest preacher's daughter really makes you feel alright.
> And the Mormon girls with the ways they kiss
> They keep their husbands warm at night.
> I wish they all could be Roman Catholic girls.

7:30 a.m. – 8:00 a.m. / Breakfast
We had a choice of a traditional American breakfast of eggs, bacon, and pancakes, or a light Italian breakfast of panini, cheese, and fruit. A key predictor for obesity in the seminary was to be found in observing who chose the American breakfast and who chose the Italian one.

<u>8:30 a.m. – 11:30 a.m. / Academic Classes</u>
Seminarians attended one or more of the universities in Rome for their theological studies. Most of us attended the Pontifical Gregorian University, a Jesuit university, and others attended the Pontifical University of Saint Thomas Aquinas, a Dominican university known as the Angelicum. Theology classes were conducted exclusively in lecture format in Italian. Depending on the professor, you might be able to ask questions, but this was not customary.

The Gregorian University—called "the Greg"—had stadium style seating where eighty to a hundred seminarians and religious might attend any particular class. There was usually a mid-morning break at 10:00 a.m. You had the choice of having a coffee at a local cafe or at the cafe in the university. Classes were conducted Monday through Saturday with Thursday and Sunday being our off days. While the schedule initially felt strange, I did enjoy the mid-week break.

We had oral exams at the midpoint and at the end of the year. At the North American College, we had developed a note-taking system in which teams of seminarians were assigned to a course, and were responsible for translating those notes into English, typing them, and copying them. Some seminarians took advantage of this system and sometimes skipped classes when they were not responsible for taking notes. This was risky because professors tended to make note of who attended classes regularly, and if, during an oral exam, the professor did not recognize you, they would ask you questions that not even God could answer.

A fascinating and disturbing aspect of oral exams was the prevalence of cheating. Many times after I exited a room from an oral exam, I would be accosted by seminarians and nuns who wanted to know the questions. I thought that their strategy was rather pointless because professors had lists of fifty to seventy-five questions, and you would be asked only three or four questions during an oral exam. The exam itself was usually only ten to fifteen minutes long. It was improbable that the same series of questions would be posed in consecutive exams, but students pursued this strategy nevertheless.

A postulant once stabbed me with her umbrella because I didn't share the questions with her. When I glared at her with my "are you kidding me" look, she replied, "Let me get this straight—you have a problem with cheating, but you don't have a problem inciting riots?"

The postulant was referring to a classroom incident that almost led to a royal rumble. When I attended class, I always sat in the seats next to the open windows because there was a broad spectrum of daily hygiene habits at the Gregorian. During a particularly windy day, Andre Caron, one of a group of seminarians from Paris, closed the windows before class began. I then got up and opened the windows. He looked at me sternly and closed the windows again.

After a few rounds of this dance, he said to me, "You Americans are obsessed with having the windows open. You are going to get us all sick. We have a serious draft coming through the windows."

I was becoming nauseated at the prospect of the windows being closed in a classroom that smelled like a skunk convention, and I shot back, "Maybe if you took a goddamned shower, I could keep the windows closed."

Andre's boys rose from their seats when they heard my words, and then Jaimie O'Halloran, a former boxer from Memphis, Tennessee, got up and volleyed at them, "Come on. I dare you to bring it. I've wanted to find a reason to fuck you guys up all semester."

The postulants and nuns stood up from their seats, eager to watch the spectacle. It was broken up when Father Bauer, a German Jesuit, entered the room and asked why everyone was standing. I asked Father Bauer if I could open the windows and he agreed.

Before Andre protested, the class broke into a chorus of laughter as I opened all the windows. As I took my seat, the American and French seminarians were glaring at each other like rival gangs.

12:00 p.m. or 5:30 p.m. / Mass

We had the choice to attend mass at either 12:00 p.m. or 5:30 p.m., depending on our academic and elective schedule.

1:00 p.m. – 2:00 p.m. / Pranzo (lunch)
This was the main meal of the day, and we were spoiled because a professional chef and a team of sous chefs were responsible for preparing meals. I would never eat that well again.

2:00 p.m. – 7:00 p.m. / Elective Activities 1
Seminarians had the choice to take academic classes, participate in apostolates (religious social service programs), do sports, explore Rome, and/or meet with their formation and spiritual directors. My favorite activity was being part of a running group that ran around the parks in Rome. I also loved pick-up basketball games.

7:00 p.m. / Evening Prayer
Again, we prayed the *Liturgy of the Hours*.

7:30 p.m. / Cena (dinner)
We usually had a very light meal: panini with cheese and deli meats, and fruit. Many of my family and friends in the US assumed that I would gain a lot of weight while I lived in Rome. I lost twenty pounds on the "Mediterranean diet" before it became popular.

8:00 p.m. – 10:00 p.m. / Elective Activities 2
Seminarians did homework readings, completed their notes, watched movies, or took a stroll into Rome. I was once reprimanded by my formation advisor for providing a screening of *Angel Heart* with Robert De Niro, Lisa Bonet, and Mickey Rourke in the student lounge. If you've seen this movie, you'll understand why I got into trouble.

10:00 p.m. / Night Prayer
There was an expectation that you go to bed after night prayer, but some did venture into the city for adventures.

12:00 a.m. / Curfew
The front gate and doors were locked. You were expected to be in your room by midnight. There was a seminarian, Jonas Price, who

was drunk one night and tried to climb the twelve-foot metal gate after curfew. He was able to climb the gate, but he fell and passed out. Fortunately, he was found alive the next morning.

Another interesting aspect of seminary living was that an order of nuns who lived near the seminary did our laundry. My mother had to sew the number "63" in all my clothes. We placed our white clothes in a white mesh bag and our dark clothes in a blue mesh bag. I laughed when a pair of my raggedy underwear had the rips sewn. I was very amused but deeply grateful.

Participating in apostolates was one of the core components of our priestly formation program. During our second year of seminary training, we were required to work at least three hours per week in an apostolate, or service program. I had been volunteering in a soup kitchen in Rome that was run by the Sisters of Charity, the religious order founded by Mother Teresa. I made the mistake of thinking that they would be friendly and warm. This was definitely not the case. They were tough and no nonsense. I was often berated for breaking serving protocols because I wanted to talk to the homeless clients and learn their stories as I served meals. The sisters had practical concerns about my behavior—there were long lines and people needed to be fed. I came to understand their desire to be compassionate and efficient.

Hearing the young mother's tears and cries outside my window inspired me to bring my talents to Bambino Gesù Hospital.

I was relieved when I learned that Sean and Patrick had volunteered at Bambino Gesù the previous year. They laid out the scope of work and expectations. The Suore Oblate del Santo Bambino Gesù (Oblate Sisters of the Holy Child Jesus) were a religious order responsible for the health and education of children and families served by the hospital. I was assigned to teach catechesis, or religious instruction.

When I arrived, Sister Caterina, an older nun who was very energetic, gave me a tour of the hospital. The children looked at me curiously as I passed from room to room. We arrived at a small room where Sister Caterina explained that I would hold classes. A group of seven students entered the room, ranging in age from six to eleven.

They smiled at me and when I began to speak Italian, a young girl named Carla said, "*Signor, sei scemo?*" "Mister, are you dumb?" The other kids began to laugh and Sister Caterina promptly scolded them.

I replied, "*Sfortunatamente, sono un scemo americano. Spero che tu possa essere paziente con me.*" "Unfortunately, I am a dumb American. I hope you can be patient with me."

The children began to laugh, and even Sister Caterina smiled. She explained to the children that I would be giving them religious lessons over the next few weeks.

When I returned to Bambino Gesù the following week, I came with picture books that featured stories about the Bible and the Catholic faith. We read a book about Easter, and we discussed the death and resurrection of Jesus.

Marcello, a seven-year-old boy, became very excited and asked, "Mister, was Jesus a zombie? If he was a zombie, that would be so cool."

I burst out laughing and admired Marcello's question. I replied, "I don't think he was a zombie. He didn't eat any of the disciples." The children fell over laughing.

"What did he look like?" asked Carla.

I replied, "We really don't know. The Bible says that his disciples did not recognize him."

Marcello's brain was still racing and he asked, "Wow, mister! Was he like Martian Manhunter? He can change his appearance?"

I had no idea who Martian Manhunter was, but I assured Marcello that Jesus was probably closer to Martian Manhunter than a zombie.

As I was packing up to leave, Carla ran to the doorway. As Carla greeted her mother with a hug and kiss, I recognized the young woman who had cried and screamed a few weeks ago. She was Carla's mother. They walked hand in hand back to Carla's room.

It wasn't until I saw Carla's mother that I realized that I had no idea how sick my students were. They seemed like healthy kids; their physical ailments weren't visible to me.

I asked Sister Caterina about Carla. She explained that Carla had lupus, and she hadn't responded well to chemotherapy. I asked Sister Caterina why Carla hadn't lost her hair and she replied, "She hasn't received chemotherapy for several weeks. We're waiting for her to get stronger before we start the next treatment. Her hair grew back very quickly."

During our last class before Christmas break, Carla ran up to me and asked, "Mister, can you translate this song for me?" She was carrying a small stereo cassette player and placed it on the table. Bruce Springsteen's song "Born in the USA" began to blare in the little room. Springsteen was very popular in Rome. In June of 1988, he gave a four-hour performance in Stadio Flaminio in northwest Rome. I attended the concert with several seminarians from the hospital wing. It was their gift to me when I came back from my father's funeral.

Carla needed help with the following lyrics: "Got in a little hometown jam so they put a rifle in my hand. Sent me off to a foreign land, to go and kill the yellow man."

Carla paused the tape and asked, "Mister, what does yellow man mean?"

I didn't know where to begin in explaining these lyrics to a six-year old kid. Before I could say anything, Marcello pressed "Play" and the music continued. The children began to sing the chorus, "Born in the USA! Born in the USA!"

Sister Caterina was not happy. She rushed into the room and shut off the stereo cassette player. She turned to me and yelled, "You're not in a nightclub! You're in a hospital!"

After Christmas break, I came back with gifts for the children. I had traveled to Salzburg and Vienna, Austria, with my seminary crew from the hospital wing. When I walked into the small hospital room, the students were very quiet and subdued.

Before I asked them why, I noticed that Carla wasn't present. Her chair was empty. I looked over at Sister Caterina who was standing in the doorway, and she asked me to step outside for a moment. She folded her hands in a prayer position and said, "Carla died on Christmas Day. She caught an infection and didn't recover." Sister Caterina looked down and took off her glasses. When she looked up, she was trying to hold back tears and quietly said, "Please do your best to make the children happy. You can play music if you want. Just make sure it's not too loud."

Before I could say I was sorry, Sister Caterina scurried down the hall.

As I looked at Carla's empty chair, my heart exploded in a million directions.

CANDIDACY

April 1989 / Rome Italy

"Have you been praying?" asked Cardinal William Plough.

"Yes, your Eminence, I have been praying," I replied.

Cardinal Plough studied me for a few seconds and then said, "Frank, my deepest desire is for you to be happy."

I could feel my heart breathe a sigh of relief after I heard these words.

He continued, "But I also feel a moral responsibility to help you to discern the will of God. As a cardinal, I walk in the footsteps of the apostles. I am their presence here on earth."

As Cardinal Plough got up from his chair and walked toward the window, I knew and feared what was coming—the pitch.

Cardinal Plough calmly stated, "And because I represent the apostles here on earth, I am privy to the Holy Spirit. I am compelled to see the movements of the Spirit in people and in events." Cardinal Plough proceeded to widen the blinds, and a glorious view of Saint Peter's Basilica flooded the room.

I began to shift the weight on my seat as the late morning sunlight shone on my face.

He continued, "Frank, I see the Spirit in you. The Spirit has made a home in you. I believe the Spirit is calling you to be a priest for His Holy Church."

Cardinal Plough had traveled to Rome to attend Candidacy, a ceremony that included a mass and a rite when the Church recognized individual seminarians as being worthy candidates for priestly ordination. Candidacy occurred at the end of the second year of theological studies and during the diaconate when candidates became permanent deacons. Candidacy was essentially the equivalent of an engagement announcement. Since I was completing my second year in Rome, I was expected to participate in the ceremony.

In February of 1989, I had written a letter to Cardinal Plough, notifying him that I would not be participating in the rite of Candidacy because I planned to leave the seminary at the conclusion of the school year.

Cardinal Plough arrived a couple of weeks before the ceremony. My formation advisor, Father Doug Maguire, informed me that Cardinal Plough wanted to meet with me in his suite at the North American College. Cardinal Plough was staying in the penthouse floor of the seminary that was reserved for cardinals and bishops. His particular suite had the most striking views of Saint Peter's Basilica and Vatican City.

When I asked Father Maguire whether I could bring someone with me, he smiled and replied, "No." When he noticed the concern that flashed across my face, he added, "Frank, it's going to be alright. Just speak from your heart, son."

Cardinal William Plough served as the leader of the Archdiocese of Boston. I first met him in 1984, during my first year of undergraduate studies at Saint John's Seminary. He had just been named Archbishop of Boston. The following year he was elevated to the College of Cardinals. He was a graduate of Harvard University, and he was celebrated for his role in advancing the Civil Rights movement in the 1960s, when he was serving as a priest in Mississippi. He took a special interest in me because I was one of the few Latinx candidates for the Archdiocese of Boston. He spoke Spanish because his father was an Air Force colonel and was stationed in military bases across Latin America. With the growing Latinx population in Boston, he wanted to be known as the cardinal who groomed Latinx priests. For Cardinal Plough, I was the future.

My interactions with Cardinal Plough were few and serious, but there were times that I pushed for levity. At a dinner in Rome with priests and seminarians from Boston, we were discussing the Episcopal Church's decision to ordain its first woman as bishop. During the conversation, I asked Cardinal Plough whether he was going to ask her out on a date. The chatter at the table came to an abrupt silence after I asked the question. He paused, smiled at me and said, "Could you set it up?"

The table broke into laughter, but some of my fellow Bostonians resented me. They wondered why and how I could get away with saying and doing certain things. Peter Jenkins, a Harvard graduate who was also studying in Rome for the Archdiocese of Boston, said to me, "When you say this bullshit, you're like fucking Audrey Hepburn. Everyone thinks it's so sweet and endearing. If I said it, people would look at me like I was Charles Manson."

Now, as I stared out of the window of his suite to take in the beautiful view of Saint Peter's Basilica, Cardinal Plough was waiting for my response. I stood up abruptly because the chair I was sitting on felt like it had sunken to the floor.

"You can sit on the couch if you want. Those chairs are pretty old," the cardinal said as he chuckled.

The couch was a little firmer, and I was no longer staring into the glare of the sun.

"Your Eminence, I appreciate your faith in me, but I don't believe I can be a priest. What I've discerned so far is that the Spirit is inviting me to move in a different direction."

He frowned when I said this and replied, "Frank, why would God bring you to Rome only to slip the rug out from under you? Don't you see the larger divine movement in your life?"

"Yes, I do see the movement, but I don't think it's linear. My experience of God is that our paths are always winding, and the way ahead is never clear. It's a matter of trusting that we're walking the path."

Cardinal Plough shook his head and said, "Look, I've been in this rodeo a little longer than you have. I know something about how God operates. God calls us to participate in His salvific mission to heal the world. There is no greater calling than the priesthood to heal. You are a healer Frank. I can see this clearly in you. Can you see it?"

I looked at my hands and wondered if I could still heal without being a priest. I finally decided to roll the grenade into the room: "Your Eminence, I'm in love. I would not be able to fulfill the requirements of celibacy."

He ran his hand through his thick white hair and smiled. "Frank, I fall in love all the time. This is natural in the life of a priest. It doesn't mean you don't have a vocation. It means you have an open heart. An open heart is the perfect vessel for God."

I smiled when he said this. I wondered whether he had ever fallen in love. From our brief interactions, I suspected that he may have been in love with himself. "Your Eminence, I know that you and the Archdiocese have invested a lot in me. I'm not making this decision on a whim. I love the priesthood too much to be cavalier about this decision."

Cardinal Plough looked down at his episcopal ring and, as he twisted it, he asked, "Are you considering marriage? Marriage is a sacrament. You can live a sanctified life through marriage."

I was wondering where he was going with this.

"The problem I see, Frank, is that I don't think you will ever be satisfied living a normal life. I'm not saying that you don't love this person. Am I correct to assume this is a woman?" he asked.

"What would you do? Do you have another passion besides this woman? I'm posing these questions not to discourage you, but to challenge you to go deeper."

To his credit, he was raising legitimate points. I knew priests who had fallen in love, but they made the choice to remain celibate because the priesthood was their path to a deeper love, a love that partner relationships could never fully satisfy. And I knew I loved Sophie, but I had no clue what I wanted to do with my life. Being a priest had been my sole dream for so many years. I didn't have another dream.

"Frank, this is what I propose: You should participate in the ceremony this coming Sunday. You are not being ordained. You are simply making a statement that you are open to ordination. You can still leave at the end of the year if you feel the same. Why close yourself off to the possibility that God is calling you to serve Him?"

He showed me the exit, and I should have walked through it, but I didn't. I was becoming angry because he didn't appear to care about my perspective or my thoughts or my feelings. He seemed not to care for me as a person. I was simply an asset. It felt like he was a bully in religious garb.

I shared my final reflection about my decision, "Your Eminence, I take the rite of Candidacy very seriously. I am not going to give a public proclamation to a lie. I've made my decision. I need to trust that it's the right one. If I cannot trust my conscience, I could never make a good priest."

Cardinal Plough looked at me and extended his hand, "Frank, I want to continue the conversation. I will honor your decision not to participate in the rite of Candidacy, but I want to be clear that more work needs to be done to discern God's will."

We never had the opportunity to continue the conversation. In addition to the letter that I had sent to Cardinal Plough, I formally announced to the seminary faculty and students that I was leaving. I posted a letter on the community bulletin board that hung on the first floor outside the refectory. The bulletin board served as our social media. My life in the seminary changed those last three months. I was still going to chapel and class. I was still socializing and playing sports. The difference was that I had become invisible. Even in my hospital wing community, I felt like an outsider.

As for Cardinal Plough, I learned years later that he had escaped to Rome in the wake of the sexual abuse crisis that exploded in Boston in the early 2000s. He died in Rome in 2017.

May 1989 / Rome, Italy

When Candidacy Sunday finally arrived, I sat in a pew at the back of the chapel. I saw my classmates dressed in white albs, waiting in the back of the center aisle for Candidacy to commence. Jack Donovan looked over at me, winked, and playfully gave me the finger. As seminarians populated the chapel, they politely avoided sitting at my pew.

Just before the ceremony started, I saw Francesca standing in the back, surveying the chapel. She was wearing a stunning knee-length, asymmetrical red dress that hugged her body tightly. I thought it was incredibly ironic that the red hue of Francesca's dress matched the color of Cardinal Plough's red vestments.

When Francesca found me in the back, she waved. As she sat down, she leaned into me and proudly whispered, "*Chiunque vorrebbe scoparmi con questo vestito.*" "Anyone would want to fuck me in this dress."

I would typically laugh at Francesca's crazy comments, but in this case, I didn't. When Francesca saw my muted reaction, she squeezed my hand firmly and said very slowly and deliberately, "I promise you everything will be alright."

I smiled gratefully and said, "Thank you for being my angel in red."

She laughed and replied, "*Non sono un angelo signore. Ma ti ringrazio.*" "I am not an angel, mister. But I thank you."

As Francesca adjusted her dress, I thought about the critical role of women in Jesus' life. In his final moments, everyone had abandoned Jesus except for a courageous contingent of women disciples. They witnessed his death, buried his body, and were the first witnesses to his resurrection. I looked over at Francesca and realized that she was supporting me in the same vein. I was not certain about her intentions, good or bad, but she did stand and sit with me during a very difficult hour. An atheist had a very special place in my heart.

SHOWER CURTAIN

September 1988 / Rome, Italy

I missed Sophie terribly, and I wasn't in a good space. Seminarians and faculty were returning to the North American College (NAC) and sharing about their summer adventures. I wasn't ready to talk about my summer romance with Sophie. I was anxious about being the object of scorn for not honoring my celibacy commitment. I felt incredibly alone. After I had bought the necklace for Sophie, I was solidifying my decision not to be an ordained priest, and I decided to notify seminary leadership. I scheduled a meeting with Monsignor Timothy Walker, the rector of the NAC.

Monsignor Timothy Walker had served as a priest in the diocese of San Diego before he became the rector of the NAC. He was fortyish with perfectly styled hair that had different shades of grey, reminding me of actor Alan Thicke from the 1980s sitcom Growing Pains. Monsignor Walker carried himself in a casual but dignified way. He bore the brunt of some criticism in the seminary because a number of faculty and priests wanted the rector to be a stern disciplinarian who whipped boys into men. His model of leadership was more detached and cerebral.

When Monsignor Walker met with me, he first tried to engage in small talk. I was never good with small talk. When he realized that I was getting uncomfortable, he asked how he could help. I jumped right into it and informed him that I needed to leave the seminary. I was surprised by the definitive tone of my words—I was nervous. The reality was that I was still struggling with the decision, but I didn't present it as a struggle. On some strange level, my heart was speaking and my mind was racing to catch up.

Monsignor Walker was surprised by my announcement and inquired about why I wanted to leave. I didn't answer his question. I shared nothing about Sophie. I was concerned that he would dismiss this relationship as a summer fling, and he would encourage me to stay. I made no attempt to explain how my understanding of the priesthood was evolving. From my perspective, the ordained priesthood was no longer aligned to my personal and professional identity. I didn't really tell him anything—except that I wanted to leave. My feeling at the time was that I didn't want to deal with saying something that could later incriminate me. I was thinking about my father and the nightmare he endured for many years for telling the truth about who he was and what he desired.

I was surprised that Monsignor Walker did not press me for my reasons for leaving. He simply asked when I wanted to leave. I told him that I wanted to leave Rome as soon as possible. He instructed me to write a formal letter stating that I was leaving the seminary and outlining the reasons why. He wanted my letter by the end of the day.

I went to my room and sat down at my manual typewriter. I stared at the blank page for an hour, and then I decided to walk out into the city for some air. As I was leaving the seminary, I ran into Monty Nichols, a classmate from Denver, Colorado. I must have been wearing my anguish on my face because he immediately invited me to join him for a beer in the city. We walked to Trastevere, a beautiful bohemian section of Rome that had great artisan shops, craft beer, bakeries, and trattorias. Walking to Trastevere was a daily ritual in the seminary. We loved buying freshly-made cornetti (Italian croissants) and watching movies at the Cinema Pasquino.

As we were drinking beer, Monty took off his glasses and wiped them with a napkin. He talked like a surfer dude, "Frankie, I know that something is up. Tell me what's weighing you, brother."

I liked Monty but I was never close to him. I was weighing whether to talk with him about Sophie.

"Oh come on, brother. You'll feel better when you spill the beans," Monty implored.

I finally told him the story about Sophie. He listened intently and adjusted his glasses at various points during my story. When I finished, we sat in silence for a while and sipped on our beers.

"I think it's awesome. I really do. Have you told anyone else?" Monty asked.

"No," I lied. I didn't tell him that I had talked to Francesca about Sophie. I didn't know how Monty felt about Francesca. She was dismissed as a crazy flirt by a number of my classmates. I felt comfortable talking about Sophie with Francesca because she operated outside the seminary system, and I knew that she wouldn't judge me. She was also a good friend and I trusted her. I wasn't sure whether or not I trusted Monty.

"Wow, man. This is a virgin confession. I'm honored, man. Thank you for trusting me. Do you want me to give you absolution?" He laughed and continued, "What you need, Signore, is a trip. You're carrying some heavy shit. You need to get some sun. Drink some limoncello. And just relax."

Monty proposed Positano, the mecca vacation destination for priests and seminarians at the North American College. Positano was a small cliffside city in Salerno that was a four- to five-hour train ride from Rome. It was located on the Amalfi coast, and it reminded me of Greece. I resisted going to Positano because I was annoyed that it seemed to be the only destination of interest in the seminary. I knew it was beautiful from photos, but I didn't understand the Positano obsession. When Monty proposed Positano, I smiled and said, "Of course."

I went back to the seminary to write the letter. I stared at the typewriter, and the only words I was able to tap out were "Dear Monsignor Timothy Walker." I decided to go to the Chapel of the Word; it was a small chapel in the seminary that had an open Bible on a small altar. A number of seminarians didn't like the chapel because it didn't have a tabernacle, a sacred box that holds consecrated bread believed to be the Body of Christ. I enjoyed the intimacy of the small chapel, and I knew it would be empty because it was so unpopular.

As I sat in the chapel, I thought about how much I loved the priesthood. I loved it because I could serve as a channel for love, compassion, and healing. I had absolutely zero interest in the Catholic corporate ladder of becoming a pastor, monsignor, bishop, cardinal, or pope. I was chosen to be sent to Rome by the faculty at Saint John's Seminary College, where I did my undergraduate studies.

Some of my classmates resented that I had been chosen. For four years they had expressed their desire to go to Rome because they believed it was a fast track to being a monsignor or a bishop. I never shared that desire, and I was absolutely surprised the day I was invited to complete my studies in Rome. The faculty gave me forty-eight hours to think about it. My decision to go had more to do with Frederico Fellini films—I was excited at the prospect of living in Rome. I was approaching priesthood the way Spiderman embraced his superhero identity: I just wanted to be your friendly neighborhood priest.

When I returned to my room, I pulled the page from the typewriter and threw it in the trash bin. I then walked to Monsignor Walker's suite. I knocked on his door and told him that I had decided to stay. He smiled and said, "I've always found that when I write things, things become clearer."

September 1988 / Positano, Italy

During our train ride to Positano, Monty peppered me with questions about Sophie and the feelings I had about our relationship. His relentless questioning was bordering on pathological. At one point, I told him to stop. Monty looked hurt and replied, "Just trying to be here for you, brother. What you need is some catharsis. And you need it in a serious way."

I thanked Monty for his concern, but I told him that I needed some space and assured him that catharsis would happen in its own time. Monty was sitting across from me on the train, and I took out a book from my backpack and began to read it intently. I kept rereading the same page but nothing registered. I was too focused on avoiding a conversation with Monty. Monty asked if I enjoyed the book. I lied about my interest and continued pretending that I was into the book.

When we arrived at Positano, I understood why this small city was so hyped. The whitewashed stucco and tile buildings lodged in the mountain cliffs looked like an ornate wedding cake. The coastal water was bluer than blue. Monty must have noticed my look of awe because he slapped me on the back and said, "Are you liking, Frankie?"

We stayed at a small pensione near the coast that was popular with seminarians and priests. After a long train ride, I was looking forward to taking a shower.

The bathroom, like many European bathrooms, was very small and compact. As I tried to step into the tub, I felt like a contortionist in a circus. I was barely able to close the tangerine-colored shower curtain, and I almost fell as I reached for the handheld showerhead propped on the faucet. To use the showerhead, I had to bend down because the hose connected to the faucet was short. I tried sitting in the tub, but it was impossible to clean myself while my knees banged into my face. I was able to get up, but I had to remain stooped over. While I was trying to find the right position, I saw a pair of eyeglasses peering through a small slit in the shower curtain where the ends met. I aimed the showerhead at the slit and sprayed water toward the eyeglasses.

After I sprayed water through the slit of the shower curtain, I heard a loud gigglish laugh that sounded like the Joker. I yelled, "Monty, what the hell are you doing?"

There was no response. I almost banged my head on the floor because I slipped as I jumped out of the tub. I went to dry off and wrapped a towel around my waist. When I went into the small bedroom, Monty was sitting on the bed smiling.

I asked Monty, "What were you doing? I saw your glasses through the curtain."

Monty tackled me and began tickling me. The towel had flown off me and Monty yelled, "Let's see how ticklish Frankie is!"

I elbowed Monty in the face and knocked off his glasses. He jumped up and said, "Fuck, you almost broke my nose! I was just fucking around. Chill, brother."

I grabbed the towel to cover myself. As I got dressed, I yelled, "Stay the fuck away from me." Monty came over to hug me, but I pushed him away.

Monty yelled back, "You're a fucking homophobe. I was just playing around. You're like all those other fucking homophobes at NAC!"

I grabbed my backpack and headed out of the pensione. Monty followed me and asked what he needed to do to make it right. I ignored him and kept walking. When I turned around, I saw that he had collapsed on the narrow street.

He was lying on his back crying, and he kept repeating, "I'm sorry. I'm sorry. I'm sorry."

Some tourists came up to him to see if he was alright. I was thinking to myself that I should just keep going, but I walked back. I handed him his glasses that had fallen off and helped him up.

He kept repeating that he was sorry as he followed me to a cafe, where I sat down. Monty sat across from me and said, "I'm pressing rewind. Can we please start again?"

I looked down and replied, "I don't know, Monty. Are the rumors about you true?"

A glare eclipsed his troubled face when I asked about the rumors. I had heard that Monty had received a hate letter from a fellow seminarian because of his sexual exploits both inside and outside the seminary. One of the rumors was that my Boston classmate, Peter Jenkins, had written a scathing letter demanding that he leave the seminary. I tried my best to avoid gossip because life at the seminary was challenging enough.

Monty replied, "It's all bullshit. So many of the guys at NAC are so fucked up. You know that."

I did know that. I didn't think that "many" was the right descriptor, but I estimated that about 10 percent of the seminary population had serious emotional issues. We did have access to professional therapy through the seminary but, unfortunately, the ones who needed it the most rarely asked for support.

"You didn't answer my question. Are the rumors true?" I asked.

"I'm not a fucking sex offender, if that's what you mean." Monty replied.

"Then explain what happened." I insisted.

"The point of this whole fucking trip was to have fun. To unwind. To let go of the bullshit." Monty replied.

"So being a Peeping Tom and committing sexual assault is unwinding?" I tried to ask calmly.

Monty slammed the table, and a bottle of aqua minerale fell and crashed to the floor. He then yelled, "Are you fucking judging me? People have judged me my whole life! They're sick and they're trying to convince me that I'm sick! Is that what you're trying to do?"

The waiter came over to clean up the shards of broken glass. I apologized and paid for the bottle. I left the table and walked towards a taxi. Monty stayed at the cafe. I took the taxi to Naples and bought my ticket for the next train to Rome.

When I returned to the seminary, I had thought about reporting the incident to the rector, but I decided against it. I felt embarrassed and ashamed about what had transpired. I buried the incident in my mind and heart like many victims do. When the sexual abuse crisis exploded in the year 2000, and revealed the pervasive problem of sexual abuse within the institutional Catholic Church, I wondered whether I had made the right decision.

I learned years later that Monty Nichols was convicted in 2007 of two counts of sexual assault on a male teen when he served as pastor of a Catholic church in Colorado. He is currently serving a sentence of fourteen years to life, and was eligible for parole in 2019.

SORROWFUL MYSTERY 5

LAST SUPPER

June 1989 / Rome, Italy

I took off my shoes and socks, rolled up my pants, and stepped into the clear and cold water of the Fontana dei Quattro Fiumi in Piazza Navona. It had always been my favorite fountain, and I wanted to see it because it was my last day in Rome. I was excited to return home and see Sophie, but I was feeling melancholic about leaving Rome. I placed my hands on the horse at the base of the fountain and pressed my cheek against its neck. "I'm going to miss you, my friend. Take care of the others," I said as I stroked the neck made of travertine stone.

It was 5:30 a.m., and I wanted to soak in the city for one last day. I headed to the Campo de' Fiori and saw vendors setting up the farmers market. I stood still and closed my eyes as I smelled the rolling waves of oranges, apples, and peaches. I could hear the crates opening and banging. As I was enjoying a carnival of scents, I felt someone shove me from the rear, and when I turned around, I saw Francesca.

"Do you think you're in a church? There are a thousand in Rome and you pick this place," Francesca said playfully. We had plans for a final dinner in Trastevere that Francesca coined as the "last supper."

She asked, "So are we still on for tonight? You'll love the food at my uncle's restaurant."

I told her that we were still on, but a question bubbled into my head that was completely unexpected, "Could you wear the red dress?"

Francesca placed her hands on her hips and mockingly protested, "*Cosa sono la tua puttana? Lo indosserò se indosserai i tuoi chierici sacerdoti. Affare?*" "What am I your whore? I'll wear it if you wear your priest clerics. Deal?"

I agreed to wear my priest clerics; at least I had found some use for them.

June 1989 / Boston, Massachusetts

I took a red-eye from Rome to Boston. As the plane took off from Fiumicino International Airport, I looked out the window for a final view of Rome. As I sat back in my seat, I wondered whether my homecoming would be as beautiful as I had imagined it in my dreams. I was nervous about the possibility of being disappointed.

It had been a strange last three months in Rome. I felt disconnected from my classmates because of my problem of invisibility. I also felt disconnected from Sophie. We had been writing to each other at least once a week and sometimes twice a week. Over the last three months, however, I had only received three letters from Sophie. I didn't know what this meant. I concocted the excuse that she had been busy because she was preparing to graduate from UMass and was steeped in planning for life after graduation.

As the plane was landing, I enjoyed the view of the Boston skyline. I didn't realize how much I had missed it until I saw it. I exited the gateway and saw a small group of people waving and jumping up and down: my mother; my sister, Marie; her boyfriend, Matt; my brothers, Anthony and Andrew—and Sophie.

Sophie was wearing waist-high, acid-washed jeans and a purple turtleneck blouse. She beamed an incandescent smile, wrapped her arms around me, and held me for what felt like hours but was only a few seconds. She was wiping the tears from her eyes and said, "I cannot believe that you're finally here."

We walked hand in hand as we went to fetch my luggage from the baggage claim. As we were walking, I glanced at her profile, and she looked as beautiful as when I first saw her in Doña Teresa's apartment. My time with Sophie in Salamanca had felt like a dream, and I was relieved that it had been real. I couldn't wait to give her my gift, and I pulled the box out of my backpack. When she opened it, her mouth gaped in awe as she looked at the Venetian glass necklace. She placed it around her neck. She gave me a big hug and told me that it was perfect.

My brothers placed my luggage in the family station wagon, and we headed to my mother's home in Stoneham, about ten miles north of Boston. My mother had prepared her popular dish of lasagna and meatballs, along with a Neopolitan cake that consisted of a marbled vanilla and chocolate cake with fresh strawberries and jello.

After lunch, Sophie and I decided to go for a walk. I lived a short distance from Stoneham High School, and I suggested that we walk toward the school. Sophie loved the horse farm that we passed along the way and asked if I knew how to ride. I told her that I used to ride my grandfather's horses in Honduras, but I was pretty rusty. As we walked up the long driveway of my high school, it felt surreal to be with Sophie. I was not only painfully shy of women in high school; I was afraid of them.

I asked Sophie if we could walk toward the football field. As we entered the field, I ran to the fifty-yard line and began to wave my arms up and down, encouraging the imaginary crowd of fans to cheer. Sophie laughed as I was flapping my arms. I felt for the first time in my life that I had won. I was the winning quarterback who threw the Hail Mary pass. I was the point guard who scored the winning basket at the buzzer. I was the footballer who did the miraculous bicycle kick to win the World Cup. I was the runner who broke the course record at the Boston Marathon. I was Bobby Orr flying through the air after scoring the winning goal for the Stanley Cup. I was Carlton Fisk waving his arms to will his World Series Game 6 home run to stay fair as it hit the foul pole of the Green Monster at Fenway Park. I was the guy who got the girl. And it felt good. It felt really good.

June 1989 / Rome, Italy

As I was walking to Trastevere to meet Francesca for dinner, I felt a little self-conscious being dressed in my priest clerics. Typically I would change into my street clothes when venturing out to Rome at night. Some seminarians wore their clerics out at night, thinking they could score a free meal. I loved the sights and sounds of Trastevere: artists displaying their work and the aroma of freshly cooked bread, pasta, and meat wafting down the street.

When I arrived at the trattoria, a middle-aged gentleman met me at the entrance and said, "You must be Francesca's friend." He had our table ready, and I munched on crostini as I waited for Francesca. I was feeling something that I didn't expect to feel—a twinge of despair.

As I was trying to understand my feelings, Francesca came through the door of the trattoria like a summer breeze. She was a vision in the red dress and somehow looked even more stunning than she had in the chapel at the North American College. I wasn't sure if it was the light or if it was the third glass of vino bianco but she looked perfect.

She asked me if I had waited long. I lied. I had waited for over an hour. She was impressed that I had the courage to wear my clerical garb and said, *"Sarai in grado di scopare qualsiasi donna tu voglia in quel vestito."* "You'll be able to fuck any woman you want in that suit."

I ordered the carbonara and Francesca ordered the bucatini all'amatriciana. These were our favorite pasta dishes, and we did a dish exchange every few minutes. I loved talking to Francesca because she liked to talk about things that mattered. We spoke of the social justice movements in Latin America and Europe. She was fascinated with NASA's space program, and we discussed the exploits of the space shuttle. We loved James Bond movies, and we discussed whether actor Timothy Dalton was a good Bond (we agreed that he was). Maybe these things didn't matter to other people, but they mattered to us.

Francesca then asked, "Are you looking forward to seeing Sophie?"

I had avoided talking about Sophie with Francesca for months. She had never expressed jealousy, but I had stopped talking about her.

"Yes, I've missed her a lot this past year." I replied.

"And how has the communication been between the two of you?"

"We've been writing letters to each other, and about twice a month we'll talk on the phone." I didn't tell Francesca that Sophie hadn't written to me that often over the last three months.

"Do you still feel the same about her? Are you still in love with her?" Francesca flashed a mischievous smile as she asked this.

"Yes. I do love her, and I am still in love with her."

Francesca wiped her mouth with her napkin. I wondered whether she was jealous. A part of me wanted her to be jealous. She looked up with a concerned expression and said, "I hope it works out for you. Love can be a bitch. Just like the song by the Scottish group [Nazareth], 'Love hurts, love scars, love wounds and marks.' I would tell you to be careful, but no matter how careful you are, love can fuck you."

"Have you ever been in love, Francesca?" What I really wanted to know was whether she was in love with me.

"Only once. But the boy never noticed me." Francesca replied with a nervous smile.

Francesca's response piqued my curiosity. Since she had once advised me that I should fuck as many women as possible, I was curious about what she really thought about love—what she thought about me.

"Francesca, do you believe the things that you say about love and sex? I know that you're often joking, but sometimes I'm not sure."

"I am bullshiting exactly 97.3 percent of the time. You know I enjoy torturing the celibates. I am a priestess of the real. I worship at the altar of science, reason, and sex."

"Who was the boy you loved?" I asked. I was pressing her for a confession. I didn't know whether I was the boy she loved. If she did confess her feelings to me, I wouldn't know how to respond. I did love Francesca on some level, but I was in love with Sophie. I felt conflicted and guilty about emotionally betraying Sophie. It felt strangely like my night with Lucía in Salamanca.

Francesca adjusted her dress and took a sip of her wine. "The past is the past. I don't have access to a time machine. I believe the past should always stay in the past." She wasn't going to crack, and I felt a mixture of admiration and relief.

"Do you think you'll ever marry or fall in love?" I stubbornly asked. My curiosity was trumping my fears about her feelings for me.

"I have a 32.7 percent chance of falling in love. I haven't done the calculation for marriage."

I was really frustrated by her evasions. "I'm serious Francesca. Could you drop your act just for a few minutes? I do love your performances. You are a walking Fellini film, but I really want to know what you believe about love."

At this point, it was my pride that was pressing her more than love. I just wanted to know whether she felt anything for me. I loved Francesca, but I would not have been able to overcome the guilt of betraying Sophie if I were to confess my feelings for her.

Francesca smiled at me nervously and asked what we should order for dessert.

August 1989 / Wenham, Massachusetts

I heard the burgers being plopped on the grill and they began to sizzle over the open flame. Eddie, Sophie's brother, was manning the grill, and he asked me if I wanted cheese on my burger. Sophie's parents had invited me to join them for an evening barbecue. They lived in Wenham, a town that was a twenty-five-minute drive northwest of Stoneham. It was a remarkable example of serendipity that I met Sophie over three thousand miles away in Spain and grew up just eighteen miles away.

I had been home for almost two months. Sophie and I had seen each other almost every day. She was reclining on a beach chair in the backyard while Eddie was grilling. I was sitting on a white plastic chair next to her, sipping on a bottle of beer. When I asked Sophie what she wanted to do after dinner, she replied, "I am so fucking bored."

Mrs. Anderson, Sophie's mother, reminded her that she didn't like crude language. Mr. Anderson called us for dinner, and we sat at a picnic table on the patio deck. Sophie's parents asked about my plans now that I was home. I told them that I was thinking about entering a master's program in philosophy at Boston College.

"What are you going to do with that?" asked Sophie. She was annoyed with my answer.

"That's wonderful," said Mrs. Anderson. "It will give you some time to figure out what's next."

June 1989 / Rome, Italy

The waiter brought the dessert out to our table: a crostata di frutta—a fresh fruit tart with cream and mixed berries. Francesca and I shared the fruit tart, and I ordered a small *caffè*. Like a master magician, Francesca continued to escape my questions about love and marriage. I decided not to press her anymore.

I walked Francesca to her apartment. Some elderly Italian ladies dressed in black expressed their displeasure that Francesca and I were walking arm in arm. When we arrived at the entrance to her apartment, she gave me an abrupt kiss on the lips and turned quickly to open the door. Before I could thank her for everything, she stood at the doorway and said, *"La nostra ultima cena è stata perfetta. Non voglio rovinarlo con sentimentalismo."* "Our last supper was perfect. I don't want to ruin it with sentimentality." She blew me a kiss and closed the door.

I stood outside Francesca's doorway for a few minutes. I looked up and noticed that a second floor light had come on. I hoped that she would come to the window. She never did. I walked back to the seminary thinking about Francesca. I was deliberating about whether I should have said something to Francesca about my feelings for her. I thought about going back and knocking on her door, but I decided against it. I rationalized that I was leaving Rome anyways.

As I passed a vendor selling fruit on my way to seminary, I regretted not saying anything to Francesca.

That was the last time I would see Francesca. About ten years after I had left the seminary, I traveled to Rome to look for Francesca, but I wasn't able to find her. Her family had apparently moved from the area. I want to believe that she's happy because she deserves all the happiness in the world.

August 1988 / Wenham, Massachusetts

After we had dinner with her parents, Sophie and I walked through a wooded area near her home. She began to cry, and I asked her what was wrong. Sophie replied, "It's over Frank. We're over."

I was confused and I asked her what she was talking about. She continued, "Frank, I met a guy at UMass. His name is Ethan. He kept asking me out, and I kept telling him 'no.' It's just—you were away for so long. I didn't think this would happen. I have feelings for Ethan. I've been thinking about him. I'm sorry, Frank. I didn't want this to happen."

I was in shock and the feelings of devastation began to seep into my heart. I was also angry. I had sacrificed so much to be with Sophie—my dream of being a priest and my love for Francesca. Devastation and rage were twisting within me like a monstrous vine in a nightmare. And I was waiting to wake up.

I stopped walking but Sophie kept walking. She never looked back. I ran to catch up with her, and she finally acknowledged me. "I haven't said anything to my parents. Could you tell them goodbye and just leave?" Sophie didn't look at me when she made this request.

I didn't say goodbye to her parents or to her brother Eddie. I got into my mother's stationwagon and drove home.

This wasn't the last time that I would see Sophie. Over the next two years we reconnected multiple times, trying to recapture the magic that we had in Salamanca.

GLORIOUS MYSTERIES

Be like the sun for grace and mercy. Be like the night to cover others' faults. Be like running water for generosity. Be like death for rage and anger. Be like the Earth for modesty. Appear as you are. Be as you appear.

~ Rumi

GLORIOUS MYSTERY 1

PATHWAYS

August 1991 / Chelsea, Massachusetts

I rang the buzzer next to the large metal double doors. I waited for
a few seconds longer and pressed the buzzer again. There was still
no response. I stood back from the doors to see if I could see anyone
through the windows. I was standing in front of Chelsea High School
in Chelsea, MA, the week before Labor Day in 1991.

Chelsea is an immigrant city occupying an efficient area of 2.2
square miles. At that time, the city had a growing Latinx population
and was one of the most densely populated cities in the state—and the
smallest in terms of area. Chelsea was experiencing a steep economic
downturn and had gone bankrupt earlier in the year. The governor
of Massachusetts appointed a state receiver to stabilize the city's
finances and operations. Chelsea had imploded after years of mob rule
and political corruption—two previous mayors had been convicted
of federal crimes. Because of the city's financial straits, there was a
question whether Chelsea would be able to open its public schools in
September of 1991. The governor had asked Boston University to take
over management of the Chelsea Public School system.

As I was waiting at the entrance of the school, I heard a loud
clanging. I could hear that someone was trying to open the metal
doors from the other side. The door popped open and a thirtyish-year-
old woman welcomed me inside. Madison Johnson was the director

of a new pilot program at Chelsea High School called the Pathways School. I was struck by Madison's appearance; she didn't look like the teachers I had in high school. She had short, spiky dark hair and wore a dark jacket, with black pants that flared at the thighs. Madison reminded me of the rocker Joan Jett.

We walked down a corridor that had desks piled in the hallway. I could smell the fresh wax that had been applied to the floors of the classrooms. We went to a classroom that had four desks: three in a semi-circle and one that faced the semi-circle. Two people walked up to greet me. Clare Walsh extended her hand to welcome me. She reminded me of a much younger Sister Caterina, the nun from Bambino Gesù Hospital in Rome. Clare was petite with grey hair and wire frame glasses. Victor Santos gave me a firm handshake and in a deep voice said, "Welcome, brother." He was built like a wrestler and wore layers of gold chains around his neck, baggy pants, and a New York Yankees baseball cap. Victor was from Puerto Rico and had recently graduated from Chelsea High School. He was working on an associate's degree in counseling at Bunker Hill Community College. Victor invited me to sit at the desk that faced the semicircle.

I was interviewing for a history teacher position at the Pathways School. Students and staff had shortened the name to "Pathways" when referring to the school. Pathways was a grant-funded program through RJR Nabisco, a tobacco and food conglomerate. RJR Nabisco had awarded $18.5 million to fifteen schools across the country to incubate innovative approaches that would radically change teaching and learning practices. The grant was phase one of the Next Century Schools initiative that encouraged public school systems to engage in sustained creativity and innovation. Pathways had autonomy in budget, staffing, and curriculum. The hope was that these pilot schools would demonstrate that autonomy from traditional bureaucratic practices in public education would yield more positive student outcomes, in terms of academic performance, graduation rates, and college enrollment.

Given Chelsea's precarious financial situation in 1991, it was a miracle that I had an opportunity to interview for a teaching job. The city had laid off three hundred teachers before the school year had started because of the budget shortfall. Because of the budget and staffing autonomy granted to Pathways by the terms of the grant, the school was not required to hire staff from the laid-off pool. I was entering into a political hornet's nest and I had no clue.

Madison, Clare, and Victor opened their notebooks with the precision of a synchronized swimming team and began their interview. They asked me about my background and work experiences, and then they asked me more specific questions:

"What do you know about project-based learning?" asked Madison.

I had never heard of the term. I liked the term, and I inferred that it was learning related to a project, but I decided not to hide my ignorance. "I'm not familiar with that term," I replied.

Madison provided a brief overview of project-based learning: students posed questions that they found compelling and relevant, and they spent several months to a year investigating these questions. Their study culminated in a presentation about what they learned about their questions and themselves.

"What do you know about kids in Chelsea?" asked Victor as he rattled a pen on his mouth.

I explained that I had worked in a summer program at Bentley College (presently Bentley University) in Waltham, MA, called Upward Bound. It was a federally funded program that gave high school students in under-resourced communities the opportunity to take college classes and live in a college environment. The goal was to encourage high school students, especially prospective first-generation college students, to pursue postsecondary education.

A Chelsea-based youth organization, Choice Through Education, coordinated the Upward Bound program at Bentley College. They had hired me to teach introductory classes in sociology and philosophy and to serve as a resident assistant in the dorms. The students at Upward Bound were from Chelsea, and the Executive Director of Choice Through Education had informed me about the teaching opportunity at Chelsea High School.

My experience at Upward Bound had been life changing. I was ecstatic because I had found a professional passion beyond the priesthood. In many ways, education had become my new priesthood. I had developed a connection with students that reminded me of my days volunteering at Bambino Gesù Hospital in Rome. The resiliency of my students inspired me. They suffered from trauma related to racism, classism, xenophobia, and sexual abuse, but they remained optimistic about life, and they had deeply compassionate hearts. Like a priest, I was helping them to stay connected to their true selves.

I was hoping to land the position in Chelsea, but the problem was that I had never done any coursework in education, and I didn't have a teaching certificate.

While I was fielding questions, I noticed that Madison and Clare were smiling and kept looking down. I thought this was a clear sign that I was blowing the interview. Both of them finally burst into laughter. Victor asked them what was so funny. Madison then confessed, "Frank, it's your socks." I was sitting with my legs crossed, and when I looked down, I saw my white sports socks. I was wearing a navy blue pin-striped suit, and because my pants were a little short, the white sports socks were showing in all their glory. We broke into a second fit of laughter, and Madison did her best to bring the group back to the task at hand.

I left the interview convinced that I had no chance of landing the position. I liked the Pathways team, and I liked what I knew of the school model. I felt there was so much to learn, and I assumed that there would be another candidate who had more experience. Madison promised to call me about whether I would be offered the position or not.

July 1990 / Rockport, Massachusetts

A little over a year after I had left the seminary, I decided to rent a house in Stoneham with a high school friend. The house was a classic 1970s ranch-style home, with avocado-colored walls and an orange shag rug. A few weeks after I had moved into my new home, the phone rang on a hot and humid summer evening. I picked up the receiver, and it was Sophie.

"Frank, is this you?" Sophie asked.

"Wow, Sophie? Yeah, it's me. How are you?" I asked.

"I'm ok. It's great to hear your voice."

Speaking with Sophie felt surreal. I was in shock for the first few moments of the conversation, and then I felt a mingling of anxiety and elation. I didn't know why she had called me, but I was hoping that she wanted to be together again.

"Frank, I've really missed you. I've thought about you a lot over the last few months."

"Yeah, I've missed you too, Sophie. I can't believe it's been almost a year."

Sophie quietly stated, "I hope you don't mind that I'm calling you. I got your number from your mom. She told me that you have your own place. That's great." She paused for a few seconds and continued, "I don't blame you if you're still upset with me. I'm sorry for what happened. I was confused. I don't mean that as an excuse. It was just a confusing time."

I had been going through the stages of grief since Sophie and I had broken up. When she called, I was still in the stage of sadness and depression. I moved to a new place hoping that it would serve as a catalyst to leave the sadness behind. It didn't work—I just felt a deep sadness under a new roof.

"Can we get together to talk?" Sophie asked.

"Sure, whatever you want," I replied. I was trying to downplay my excitement, but feelings of terror were below the surface. Our breakup had been devastating for me—like rolling on shards of shattered glass. I didn't know whether I could survive another breakup.

We agreed to meet for an early dinner in Rockport, a coastal town near Gloucester known for its picturesque beaches, burgeoning arts scene, and fresh seafood. Sophie had just rented an apartment in Rockport, and we met at a seaside restaurant overlooking a harbor.

I arrived at the restaurant first. When Sophie arrived, she looked beautiful in a yellow sundress. As I hugged her, I smelled the soapy scent of fresh flowers and it reminded me of Salamanca. It felt like we had never been apart.

The conversation was smooth and easy. She briefly mentioned that she was no longer with Ethan, and she shared that he had predicted that she would return to me. On a strange level, I felt vindicated by Ethan's prediction—I was the better man. Being the better man was important at that moment, but I still felt uneasy. I didn't trust Sophie, and I could feel the sand of uncertainty shifting beneath me.

Beyond the passing reference to Ethan, we were conversing as if we had never broken up. We didn't discuss the breakup; we simply fast-forwarded to a new chapter as if we were operating a time machine. I welcomed this, hoping that it would erase the months of pain and devastation. It almost worked.

A few days later, I went to my mother's house to share my excitement about my reunion with Sophie. When I arrived, she was drinking coffee at the kitchen table with Richard Burns, a seminary classmate from Boston who had become close to my mother. After I shared my "fantastic news" that Sophie and I were back together, my mother struggled to smile, and tears were forming in the corners of her eyes. Richard looked down with a despondent expression like I had just told him that someone had died.

I grew angry with their complete lack of enthusiasm and shouted, "Whoever is not happy for me and Sophie can go to hell!"

Richard jumped to his feet and yelled, "Don't you dare talk to your mother that way! Every time that girl stomps on your heart, she has to pick up the pieces. The next time, she should just leave the pieces on the ground because that's what you deserve."

I wanted to put Richard's head through the wall. But I knew he was right. And I was terrified.

August 1991 / Stoneham, MA

As I was driving home from the interview, I looked forward to seeing Sophie. She was going to stay at my place for the night. Having just started a position as a researcher in a bio lab, she was working long hours, and I anticipated that she would arrive late.

As she slipped into my bed, she touched my shoulder to see if I was asleep. I wasn't, and I welcomed the feeling of her body next to me. She was always cold, and she wrapped her arms and legs around me to warm up. I always felt warm, and I liked the coolness of her body. In bed, we had a symbiotic relationship.

As I lay in bed and heard Sophie's quiet breathing, I thought about the porcelain nature of our relationship; it tended to break apart abruptly and glue together chaotically. Sophie was always the one who ended it. For the two years since I had left the seminary, we had been in an infinite loop where we wouldn't see each other for months, and then Sophie would call me and we would have an intense reunion.

The next morning, I received a call from Madison informing me that they wanted to offer me the position. Wow. Before I could even respond, Madison asked, "Could you swing by the school later today? We're going to hire you on a teacher's license waiver, and I need you to fill out some forms. We need to do this ASAP because school starts next week."

I was excited to share the news with Sophie when she returned home from work. I was still a virgin at the ripe age of twenty-seven, and I wanted to have wild sex with Sophie to celebrate the new phase of my life. Because Sophie was my first love, I had placed her on a metaphorical pedestal with the Virgin Mary and a legion of angels. I also felt a deep guilt for having given up the dream of being an ordained priest. On some emotional level, I had remained celibate as a form of penance. This was not a rational or conscious decision.

That night I was resolute in discarding the guilt and channeling my inner Don Juan, Casanova, and James Bond. I went to the local pharmacy in Stoneham to buy condoms for the first time. I was nervous and embarrassed, and I bought a ridiculous number of toiletries to hide the fact that I was buying condoms.

When Sophie climbed into my bed after another long day at work, I shared with her the news that I had been hired to be a teacher. She congratulated me, but her response was muted and I wondered why.

While we were kissing, I reached to touch Sophie, but she stopped my hand and whispered, "No. Please, no." She turned to me in tears and said, "Frank, I can't do this anymore."

I thought Sophie was referring to my strange commitment to not have sex, and I was prepared to assure her that I was committed to changing that. She told me that it wasn't about the sex, and she didn't mind not having a sex life with me. Because I didn't have the expectation to have sex with her, she believed that I really loved her. Sophie explained that the pressure to have sex was omnipresent in college and she hated it. She found it hard to trust the advances of most guys.

When I asked her to explain what was wrong, she tearfully replied, "Frank, I know you love me and I love you, but I don't think we want the same things. You seem satisfied to be a teacher or a professor, but I'm working at a career where I hope to make money. Money doesn't seem important to you, and I don't want to change you into something you're not."

I was blindsided. There had been clues, but I had refused to see them. As I was playing back our conversations in my head, I remembered when she stated in Rockport, "I want to be rich." How could I forget that? On some level, I had chosen not to hear that statement. I couldn't even remember my response.

It also struck me that we had never talked about the things that I cared about—philosophical ruminations about life, pressing issues related to social justice, or anything related to Boston sports. What did we talk about? We talked about nothing, simply nothing.

At that moment, I experienced a transfiguration—an epiphany—and I fell out of my bed laughing. I felt the absurdity of holding on. Sophie was right when she first told me in Salamanca that everything dies. I shared her fear of death—especially when it came to us. I was used to the Good Fridays of our relationship, and I was always fooled by the promise of Easter Sundays when we reconnected. I was now experiencing an Easter Sunday that wasn't an illusion. I had finally decided to say "yes" to death—I was ready to let go of Sophie. And I felt a new resolution to say "yes" to life.

Sophie was upset that I was laughing, and she cried out, "What the fuck is so funny?" I was lying on the side of my bed, and I couldn't stop laughing. Sophie got up and started getting dressed. My laughter grew louder when I saw that she was wearing oversized white panties; I hadn't noticed this before. She shoved her clothes into her bag and left the house.

I left the bedroom and turned on the TV in the living room. I pulled out the VHS cassette tape of my favorite James Bond film, *Dr. No*, and I began to play it. I paused the cassette tape at the iconic scene when Honey Ryder (Ursula Andress) was coming out of the sea in her white bikini, and she looked like Aphrodite, the Greek goddess of love. I went to the kitchen and pulled out a bottle of beer. After I opened it, I toasted Aphrodite.

As I was reveling in my inner James Bond, I felt a twinge of despair. The same despair I felt when I had dinner with Francesca for the last time. I didn't understand what it was, but the truth was flowing from my heart and seeping into my consciousness. This wasn't the first time that I had toasted Aphrodite; in fact, I was her high priest. I lived as if love were a statue—immutable and perfect. But now I was seeing the cracks on Aphrodite whenever I got close to a woman, and I didn't want to see them. I preferred my Aphrodite to be perfect.

As I looked at the image of Honey Ryder, I realized that she was my complete vision of why I had never, ever, been vulnerable with a woman. Sophie and I had never had sex in the two years since we had met. When we were in Spain, I rationalized that I was trying to salvage my commitment to celibacy—even if it was tattered. But now, I was free. Free to love and make love to whomever I wanted.

When Sophie told me that she "couldn't do this anymore," it wasn't only that we could not recapture the magic of Salamanca. She knew that we had intentionally and unintentionally built a wall between us. Our illusions, fears, and unrealistic expectations were the brick and mortar of that wall. We wanted love to be like Aphrodite, and the statue crashed on us.

I thought I was free but I wasn't. I was still a virgin, not because of a religious vow, but because I was terrified to be vulnerable—to be close to a woman with all her perfections and imperfections. I also wanted to be Aries, the Greek god of war; I wanted to be a perfect statue for her. And I didn't want her to get too close to see the cracks within me.

The problem is that marble bodies can't have sex. They can only be worshipped from a distance.

CALIFORNIA DREAMIN'

April 1992 / Charlestown, Massachusetts

A light spray of seawater kissed my face as I adjusted the angle of my oar in the water. As I tasted the saltiness of the ocean on my lips, in the distance I could see the three masts and thick oak hull of the USS *Constitution*, one of the first naval ships commissioned by President George Washington. My student Pedro yelled playfully, "Hey Frank, are you ok? You've been catching crabs all afternoon." Pedro Machado was serving as the coxswain of our boat, a thirty-two-foot pilot gig that held six rowers. Pedro was right. I had been "catching crabs," a rowing term for when the oar gets caught in the water, usually because of flawed technique.

My flawed technique was on full display that afternoon. Pedro had been patient with me and was a good coach. He was eighteen years old and had had failing grades in elementary, middle, and high school. When he arrived at the Pathways School, I read his academic file. It was a detailed description of all of his deficits: cognitive disability, reading and writing well below grade level, ADHD (attention deficit hyperactivity disorder), behavioral issues, and not a single passing grade except for gym. Pedro was originally from Puerto Rico, and his family had moved to Chelsea when he was five. His entire educational career was marked by failure, but at Pathways, he was a super star. Pedro was small in stature, but he stood tall as Master and Commander when I saw him in the stern of the ship.

Traditional education rarely provided personalized opportunities for students to shine. Within the system, they were often defined as "the problem." Pathways was founded with a countervision: the problem was not the student but rather our inability and resistance to seeing the genius within each student. At Pathways, Pedro had the opportunity to demonstrate what he could do, and we structured our education program around his assets. Through the rowing program, we discovered that he had a natural aptitude for the technical skills needed in the maritime industry. He was also a natural leader; students and staff trusted him when he provided guidance about how to work together to move our boat as one.

June 1992 / Chelsea, Massachusetts

I was a couple of weeks away from completing my first year of teaching. I was humbled by how much I didn't know and by the love and compassion of my students and colleagues. When I was hired in August of 1991, I was becoming the cofounder of a new school and a radically new approach to educating students. When Pathways opened in September of 1991, we had fifty students. Like Pedro, these students had suffered from years of academic failure. They had dropped out of school for various reasons: economic necessity (they needed to work to support their families), unplanned pregnancy, sexual and physical abuse, alcohol and drug addiction, and depression. The student demographic reflected the rising immigrant population in the city. They were primarily Latinx, African American, Afro Carribean, Cambodian, and White (Italian and Irish). They were older high school students, ranging in ages from seventeen to twenty-one. Pathways was their last chance to get a high school diploma.

The Pathways School was located in the third-floor wing of Chelsea High School. The program ran during the afternoon and evening hours: 2:30 p.m. to 9:00 p.m. The rationale for this schedule had three main components. First, running the program in the afternoon and evening allowed us to have full autonomy over the use of space without conflicting with the day program at the high school. Second, we wanted to create a sense of community where students could interact in a more intimate setting. And third, students could use the morning and early afternoon hours to work at jobs or do internships.

Pathways had a competency-based learning program, meaning that students received credits toward graduation when they successfully demonstrated a specific skill or competency. Credits were not awarded based upon logging seat time in a classroom. This competency-based system allowed students to graduate in two years rather than four.

Our program did not have formal classes; rather, we used a project-based learning approach. Students would investigate a particular question or issue that was of interest to them. In collaboration with their advisor—a teacher—they would map out the skills and competencies they would learn by completing the project. At either the midpoint or the end of the school year (depending upon the parameters and timeline of the project), students would give presentations of their project work to professionals, parents, and community members. Students were assessed using a rubric, a performance guide that documents whether students have mastered specific competencies and made progress in areas identified for growth.

Students worked on their projects in groups or individually. Depending upon the size and scope of the project, students worked on one to three projects during the course of the year.

Teachers did not teach classes, but rather co-facilitated projects with students and supported them to develop project goals, learning activities, and timelines for completion. Teachers essentially served as project managers in collaboration with their students. At the beginning and midpoint of the school year, students and teachers would cocreate a schedule that outlined when projects were happening and which students and teachers were involved. This collaborative approach emphasized student ownership, empowering students to become agents in their own learning process.

Before the students arrived at our door, the grant that funded Pathways had described five projects that were linked to different sectors: education, health and human services, law/politics, theatre arts, and transportation. We then vetted these projects with students to gauge their interests. If none of them were appealing, we were prepared to jettison the projects and start from scratch. As we discussed project opportunities, a number of students were excited about a project related to the transportation industry—a rowing program.

I was the project advisor for the rowing program. At a staff planning meeting, I had volunteered to facilitate and lead the project. My team was relieved because while they found the project fascinating, they weren't sure about braving the elements in New England.

Because I knew nothing about rowing, we had developed a partnership with the Hull Lifesaving Museum. They ran a rowing program out of the Charlestown Navy Yard. In addition to learning the science of rowing, students would also learn about the maritime history of Boston and the Harbor Islands. We did not use the sculling boats that you might typically see rowers use on the Charles River. Students would learn to row pilot gigs: thirty-two-foot wooden boats that were popular during the eighteenth century and served as a general work boat. A pilot gig's primary purpose was to bring a pilot—a specialist who knew the complexities of a harbor—to assist ships in navigating the harbor for a safe arrival. They were also used to aid ships in distress and to transport goods into the harbor.

Every project required a community partner, not only because the complexity of the project required expertise that was beyond the capacity of our teaching staff, but also because we wanted students to become agents of their own learning. Rather than passively sitting back and listening to a teacher lecture, we wanted them to aggressively go out and find the experts who could help them with their projects. This is how learning happens outside of school.

We wanted students to have a deep understanding that learning extends beyond the walls of the classroom. This was the heart of our education revolution. As I started my teaching career, I saw so many parallels between public education and the institution of the Catholic

Church. For centuries, learning was seen as the sole domain of schools, just as faith was seen as the sole domain of the Vatican.

October 1991 / Charlestown, Massachusetts

When I brought my students to the Charlestown Navy Yard for the first time, we saw a man pulling a rope to secure a pilot gig to a harbor dock. When he saw us approach him, he raised his hands and said, "You must be the Chelsea crew."

His name was Duncan McGregor, and he was the Program Director at the Hull Lifesaving Museum. He had a towering presence and was a little over six feet tall, but he seemed taller. Duncan had a thick grey beard and spoke with a billowy baritone voice.

He was exactly how I'd envisioned Captain Ahab when I'd read the novel *Moby Dick*. I expected Duncan to exclaim at any time: "Towards thee I roll, thou all-destroying but unconquering whale; to the last I grapple with thee; from hell's heart I stab at thee; for hate's sake I spit my last breath at thee."

When I told Duncan that he reminded me of Captain Ahab, he shot back, "Do you know how many fucking times a day—excuse me kids, sorry for the foul language—I hear that?"

Duncan invited us to the adjacent USS Constitution Museum to introduce ourselves. The students were expecting to begin rowing that day, but Duncan explained that there was a lot to learn before they stepped into the boat. This was a good lesson for students—they were used to fast food, and their previous school experiences had had the same nutritional value.

In addition to the safety course that students would be required to take, we reviewed the framework of competencies they would be expected to master (our team had a series of planning meetings with the Hull Lifesaving Museum team). For math, they needed to learn statistics and probability because life on the ocean required mapping routes, studying water current patterns, and making weather predictions based upon available data. History required learning geography and economics through the study of the critical role of maritime history in relation to the development of commerce in New England and beyond. For English, they would learn narrative writing structure by reading the journals and diaries of individuals who lived during the time of wooden ships. And they would learn environmental science by studying the ecosystems of the Boston Harbor and the Harbor Islands.

When I looked over at Pedro, he shook his head and said, "I don't know, Frank. This is really heavy, man." Duncan walked over to Pedro and asked him if he knew how to make a bowline knot (typically used to tie a boat to a dock). Pedro replied that he didn't. When Duncan showed Pedro how to create the knot, Pedro was successful in making the bowline knot on his third try.

Duncan then said, "Don't overthink it. Don't over complicate it. Life on the ocean is like tying a knot. You keep doing it until you learn it. There's no shame in failing unless you're doing something really stupid to endanger the lives of your crew." Pedro smiled and Duncan stared him in the eyes and said, "You can do this, son. Just trust me."

Trust was difficult for most if not all of my students. Many of the adults in their lives had failed them. Being a part of the Pathways School was a leap of faith.

May 1992 / Chelsea, Massachusetts

We invited students to call us by our first names. This was quite a shift for most of them, and in the beginning they called us "Mister" or "Miss" before they became comfortable relating to us on a first-name basis. Students were organized into advisories—teams of ten students—with a teacher serving as an advisor.

Students had the following schedule:

2:30 p.m. – 3:00 p.m. / Advisory Check-in
Students discussed their academic and personal goals for the day. It was also a time to flag issues affecting students' emotional states that may have come up at home or at work.

<u>3:00 p.m. – 6:00 p.m. and 7:00 p.m. – 8:30 p.m. / Project-based Learning</u>
During these blocks, students worked on their personalized projects.

<u>6:00 p.m. – 7:00 p.m. / Community Dinner</u>
We had dinner as a school community every evening. Using a rotating schedule, advisory teams were responsible for cooking dinner and doing clean-up.

<u>8:30 p.m. – 9:00 p.m. / Community Meeting</u>
The community meeting was an opportunity for students and staff to share important lessons that they had learned during the day, or to discuss issues that affected the school community. We used a consensus model whenever we were developing or implementing a particular policy or practice. Students felt empowered to shape the culture and direction of the school.

Each student was also assigned an adult mentor from the local community that they would meet for dinner at least once per week. The purpose was to provide students with positive adult role models to inspire them to have bold visions for their lives after high school. Mentors would also assist students to problem-solve issues that they encountered at home, work, or school.

In June of our first year, we launched the mentor program, and my advisory was responsible for cooking dinner when the mentors met with their mentees for the first time. I was not used to cooking and my students saved me. I had been spoiled in the seminary, where I'd enjoyed freshly cooked meals every day for six years. Now, I relied on my students for guidance.

Celina Lopes, an eighteen-year-old student from Cape Verde, was in charge of the kitchen when our advisory group cooked. Her family had moved to Chelsea when she was young, and she knew how to prepare all the popular dishes from Cape Verde, Puerto Rico, and Guatemala. For student mentor night, my advisory team decided to do a traditional Puerto Rican dish of *lechón* (pork) and *arroz con gandules* (rice with pigeon beans). We used the home economics room at the school to cook dinner. The room had six electric ovens that were over twenty years old, and only three of them worked.

When my students were preparing dinner, I tried my best not to get in the way. It was very common to hear the exasperated voice of a student say, "Frank, what are you doing?" This was usually said in response to something stupid I was doing in the kitchen.

While I was watching my students work their magic, I heard a voice behind me say, "Are your students ok with the fact that you're a misogynist?"

I wheeled around and saw a beautiful woman with painted-on blue jeans and a tight black tube top. She had long flowing blonde hair and big blue eyes. Whenever I heard the Mamas and the Papas anthem "California Dreamin'," she was the image that would come to mind. She was apple pie and Chevrolet. Her name was Jessica Seavers.

"*Misogynist?* Is that how you say it, Miss? What does that mean? If it means that Frank is a disaster in the kitchen, you nailed it," Celina said.

Jessica smiled, placed her hands on her hips, and explained, "Ladies, a misogynist is someone who hates women."

Celina looked at me dumbfounded and said, "Frank is that true? Are you gay? I mean, that's totally cool. Hey, I still love you if that's how you roll. I just thought my gaydar was better than that."

Jessica burst out laughing and said, "Your teacher is not gay. I'm sure of it."

I wondered how Jessica was so sure of my sexual orientation. She probably noticed that my jaw had dropped when I had turned around to see her for the first time. I found out that Jessica was going to be a mentor to Rhonda Russo, a student in my advisory. She had hoped to meet Rhonda before the mentor dinner. Rhonda had expressed an interest in exploring the medical field, and Jessica worked as a hospice nurse. I was imagining that Jessica must have served as a fountain of youth for a lot of elderly men.

Celina walked over to me and whispered, "Frank, you really need to tap that ass. Shit, that girl is firing on all cylinders." Celina's not so subtle suggestion was reflective of the relationship we had with students. We were family and our conversations reflected this connection. Still, I was embarrassed that a student was advising me on my love life.

After the mentor dinner, Madison came up to me as we were leaving the school and asked, "What happened between you and Jessica Seavers?"

I nervously discussed the incident in the kitchen, concerned that Jessica had shared her observation that I was a misogynist.

"No, she said nothing about that. She asked for your contact info, and I told her that I would check in with you to see if you were ok with that," Madison said amusedly.

"She wants my contact info? I thought she didn't like me," I replied.

Madison quickly retorted, "Geesh, I hope you develop a better read on women. You were in the seminary for too long."

June 1992 / Manchester-by-the-Sea, Massachusetts

Jessica called me at home later and asked if I wanted to spend Saturday with her at Singing Beach, a popular beach that bordered the picturesque New England town of Manchester-by-the-Sea. She lived in Revere, and I picked her up at her apartment.

Jessica was only in my car for five minutes before she asked, "Are you a virgin?"

The car lunged forward because I had abruptly pressed on the accelerator when she asked.

"I plead the fifth," I nervously replied.

"Yeah, I knew you were a virgin when I first met you. I find it really hot. You must get blue balls all the time. Does it hurt? I imagine that you have to masturbate a lot to relieve the pain."

I continued driving in shattered silence. I was embarrassed that Jessica was probing my sex life—or lack thereof—and I didn't know what to say.

"I mean, God, you're hung like a horse, and I can't imagine not getting any. Are you a *virgin* virgin, or are you an intercourse virgin? Have you ever gotten a blow job?" Jessica calmly inquired.

As I drove, I wanted to disappear. The last woman who had spoken to me in such an overtly sexual way was Francesca.

"Am I making you uncomfortable? I heard from Madison that you had studied six years in the seminary. Did they talk about sex in the seminary? What made you want to do that? I find it fucking sexy, but I can't imagine why anyone would choose to go to a seminary."

We finally arrived at Singing Beach, and we went to the bathhouse to change. When Jessica came out of the women's changing area, she was wearing a thin white bra and white thong panties. The older women were giving her dirty looks, and teenage boys were gawking at her.

"Oh my God, Jessica, you're wearing a bra and panties?" I asked in amazement.

"I don't see the difference between a bikini and what I'm wearing. I don't see the big deal," retorted Jessica.

I thought that Francesca was a walking Fellini film, but she was a Disney movie compared to Jessica. As we laid out in the sun, Jessica asked me what my plans were for Sunday.

"I have a friend who's celebrating his first mass," I replied.

"Can I come?" Jessica sprightly asked. As I lay there thinking about it, she climbed on top of me and said, "I'll make it worth your while."

The Hulk was released, and I loved it. I was still nervous about what Jessica had in mind, but I was hoping that her plan was to walk her talk.

Jessica felt the rise in my bathing suit. "I knew you were hung like a horse," Jessica said with a mischievous grin.

June 1992 / Norwood, Massachusetts

I drove to pick up Jessica at her apartment in Revere. The mass was going to be in a Lithuanian Catholic Church in Norwood. When she came downstairs, she was wearing a suede miniskirt and a white blouse with a plunging neckline that barely covered her breasts. As she closed the door to her apartment, I covered my face with my hands and said in exasperation, "Do you know that you're going to a Catholic mass? You cannot go to mass dressed like that."

Jessica looked at me defiantly and said, "I hope you grow some balls. I thought they would be as big as your dick, but I guess I was wrong."

She stood her ground, and with reluctance, I agreed to her terms. I loved her outfit— it was sexy as hell—but I wasn't looking forward to the flack we would certainly receive.

When we arrived at the church, the old Catholic ladies had already started to throw darts with their looks as we sat down. The daggers then began to fly when Jessica leaned over to me and said in a very loud whisper, "I'm not wearing any underwear." I sat in the pew wallowing in awe, shock, and terror.

After a new priest celebrates his first mass, it's customary for him to offer an individual blessing to those who request it. Jessica and I waited in line to receive a blessing from my friend and former classmate, Father Scott Vidas.

When it was our turn to receive a blessing, Jessica interrupted Father Scott and said, "I believe that we all have the power to give blessings. I would like to give you a blessing before I receive one from you."

Then she raised her hands and prayed:

> "Mother Earth, our goddess, I ask that you align the spirit of Father Scott to your spirit. May he walk in your ways of truth and light. May he resist the temptation to violate the feminine energy that pervades our universe like so many men do. May he allow himself to be pregnant with your love and compassion. I ask this through Mother Earth, our goddess. Amen."

Jessica lowered her hands and beamed me a proud smile when she finished.

Father Scott looked at Jessica and me like we were visitors from an alien planet. He smiled and thanked us and nervously gave us his blessing. Father Scott then pulled me aside and playfully said, "I will begin praying a novena (a nine-day prayer) to Our Blessed Mother, Mary, for you and your wacko girlfriend." I wanted to protest that she wasn't my girlfriend—yet. But I let it go.

After mass, Jessica asked if she could hang out with me at my house in Stoneham. When we entered the house, she asked me where my bedroom was. She then took me by the hand and led me into the bedroom. I was terrified.

I thought my days as a virgin would be over, but I was wrong. Somehow, some way, Jessica and I did everything in my bedroom except have intercourse.

When we entered the room, Jessica began gyrating like a stripper as she slowly took off her top and miniskirt. As she stood there in her glorious nakedness, she eclipsed Honey Ryder as my vision for Aphrodite; Jessica was now my complete vision for the goddess of love. As I stared at her, Jessica asked if I was all right. I told her that everything was perfect. I was sitting on my bed and she walked over to join me. I asked her if she could stand for a few seconds more. She did a very slow pirouette and held her arms out, inviting me to worship at her altar.

She then walked backward to the corner of my room, sprinted towards me, and dove onto my bed. Jessica began to tear off my clothes and climbed on top of me.

She then asked me, "Are you ready for this?"

"I want to be," I replied.

"Look, I don't want you to feel like I'm raping you. I only want it if you want it," she said with a beautiful smile.

"I'm feeling a little conflicted. There's something about being with you that feels like I'm leaving my body," I tried to explain.

"Well that sucks. That takes all the fun out of it. Stay in your body, young man!" she cajoled. Jessica studied me for a few seconds and continued, "Look, Frank, I was sexually abused as a kid. I know something of what you're feeling. Were you ever abused?"

I sat in silence for a few seconds and then replied, "Wow, Jessica. I'm so sorry. That's horrific. I wasn't abused. I really don't know what it is."

Jessica gently squeezed my penis and it grew. "Have you ever seen a doctor or therapist? Your equipment seems to work."

"No, never have. I probably should." I replied.

"Hey, it's ok. Sex is more than intercourse. I believe in being creative anyways. We don't have to do the same fucking thing over and over again." She smiled at me mischievously and shouted, "Ladies and gentleman, let the games begin!"

And the games did begin. Jessica was our ringmaster, and she introduced me to a world that I had never imagined.

GLORIOUS MYSTERY 3

PROM DRESS

June 1993 / Chelsea, Massachusetts

I unfolded the white table cloth and handed the other side to Madison. We tossed up the table cloth until it became a billowing sail, and we let it settle on the round wooden table. It was June of 1993, and we were converting a large classroom into an elegant dining space to celebrate the first graduating class of the Pathways School.

Earlier in the day, our students had crossed the stage in Chelsea High School's gym to receive their diplomas with their classmates from the day school program. After the ceremony, our students flooded into the dining space, along with their families, wearing their red graduation robes and hats (red and black were the school's colors).

My student Celina Lopes shook me like a rag doll as she hugged me and screamed for joy like Arethra Franklin. Pedro was crying, and he pulled me close with a forearm handshake.

His mother was close behind him, a beautiful middle-aged woman with dark and delicate features, and she hugged me saying, *"Gracias por traer a mi hijo de la muerte."* "Thank you for bringing my son back from the dead."

For my entire life I've fiercely resisted crying in front of people, but I could feel myself letting go as Pedro's mom held me. I whispered in her ear, *"Gracias. Pero no hice nada. Pedro lo hizo. Él lo hizo todo."* "Thank you. But I didn't do anything. Pedro did it. He did it all."

111

I was not only crying because I was so proud of Pedro. I was crying because he had accomplished his goals in spite of me. I was crying because my students and colleagues had invited me to be vulnerable to the core. Personally and professionally, I had never felt so inept, but they loved me anyway. It was the rarest of times when I experienced true and unconditional love.

I experienced a profound shift. I thought that being an effective teacher meant being an expert and knowing the answers. But I discovered that if I was ever going to be an exceptional educator, I needed to be a learner along with my students. My students and colleagues had seen my vulnerability as a learner: my small and epic failures, my daily temptation to throw in the towel, and my resolve to just keep moving forward. I was crying because somehow we had found a way to figure it out, together.

July 1992 / Stoneham, Massachusetts

My mother called me early Saturday morning. I was always worried when she called me early because I assumed she was about to share some bad news.

I immediately asked, "Mom, is everything alright?"

"Yes, honey. Everything is fine. I just wanted to let you know that I had a wonderful time with Jessica last night."

I put down the receiver, and I rubbed my hands over my face.

"Are you there?" asked my mom.

"Yeah, mom, I'm still here. Jessica didn't tell me anything about seeing you. Why did she want to see you?" I asked.

"I met her at the Pathways mentor dinner."

I hadn't noticed that my mother and Jessica had connected during our mentor dinner. Madison had asked my mother to serve as a mentor because she was looking for Latinx role models for Pathways students.

My mother continued, "She called me a week ago and asked if we could get together for dinner. After meeting her, I was very impressed. Jessica is a beautiful young lady, and she said some nice things about you. She told me that anything that is good about a man is usually because his mother raised him well—I was flattered."

"I don't understand why I was completely out of the loop about this. Why didn't you tell me?" I asked.

"Honey, I assumed that Jessica had told you," my mother explained.

"Jessica didn't say anything to me. What did you guys talk about?"

"She told me some wonderful things about you. She admires your dedication to your students. Jessica likes that you're humble and down-to-earth. She even helped me to write a personal ad," my mother said.

"Whaaat? A personal ad? What do you mean she helped you to write a personal ad?" I asked with troubled concern.

"I told her about Kevin and my frustration that I wasn't a priority in his life," my mother explained.

Kevin Schwartz was a book dealer that my mother had been dating. After my father died, my mother had begun dating for the first time. She had married my father when she was very young and had never experienced the world of dating. My mother entertained my family and friends with stories about her dating adventures. Kevin was one of those adventures that wasn't going well.

My mother continued, "Jessica convinced me that I should be with a man who placed me on a pedestal, a man who cherished me like your father did. When I told her that I wasn't meeting that kind of man, she told me that I needed to fish in a larger pond. She asked me whether I had ever tried personal ads to meet men. When I told her I hadn't, she offered to help me."

Incredulously I asked, "And how did she help you?"

"She wrote a personal ad for me. I didn't know what to put in a personal ad. I don't like to talk about myself. Jessica really has the knack for this."

I heard a shuffle of papers and my mom continued, "Honey, this is what she wrote: 'Gorgeous and sexy Mayan princess looking for a real man who is not intimidated by a powerful woman, and who really knows how to love her.' I could never have written this personal ad on my own. When I told Jessica that I was uncomfortable using the words 'gorgeous' and 'sexy' to describe myself she said, 'Candida, men are superficial. They rely on women to feel good about themselves. It's never about you. It's all about them. If you want to reel in a man, you have to speak his language.'"

I had been deeply troubled that Jessica had seen my mom without telling me. But after hearing the smile in my mom's voice when she recounted their evening, I felt grateful for what Jessica did for my mom. My mother was, and is, an amazing woman. She deserved a man who was worthy of her.

As it turns out, Candida Rosa DeVito did experience a great love in the second act of her life. Through Jessica's personal ad, she met Paul Bennett, my stepfather. Paul reminds me of the actor John Wayne, both physically and in disposition. The movie characters Wayne played always had a gruff and no-nonsense exterior but, beneath the bravado, a deeply tender and compassionate heart. My mother had found a man who loved her as deeply as my father.

My mother was only thirty-nine years old when my father died. By the time she had met Paul, I was happy for her. This hadn't been the case a few years earlier. It was hard for me—and my siblings—to see my mom date other men. It reminded me of my father's absence. And because I was still wrestling with his death, the idea of another man replacing my father was abhorrent. By the time I met Jessica, I was making the emotional transition to seeing my mother as a woman who deserved all the happiness in the world.

April 1993 / Chelsea, Massachusetts

When we entered senior prom season, the female students in my advisory provided me with detailed updates about their search for the holy grail—the prom dress. The prom dress search could have served as a yearlong project in itself. Rhonda Russo came from a very large Italian family, and she had dropped out of school when she became a teenage mother. She had found her groove at Pathways, and she was excited about "the dress."

Rhonda explained, "You gotta understand. My family is obsessed with helping me to find the right dress. It's actually a lot of pressure. They make me feel that if I don't find the right dress, my life will be ruined."

As Rhonda was sharing her prom dress saga in our advisory circle, I looked over at Celina, who was staring at the floor. Celina had been very quiet during our advisory meeting; this was unusual. When I asked her if she was ok, she replied, "Sorry, Frank. I'm just not feelin' it today. I have a lot on my mind."

I asked Celina if she wanted to share what was weighing her down with the group, and she said, "Listen, I love you guys. I love you guys to death. It's just that I don't feel like talking right now."

When the meeting ended, I asked Celina if I could talk with her alone. We decided to take a walk outside. As we exited the building, Celina threw her arms around me and began to cry convulsively. I gently asked her what was going on.

When she regained her composure she explained, "There's just a lot of shit going down. My mother left me and my brother, Freddie. She's following her boyfriend back to Cape Verde. Fuck—she didn't even say goodbye. She left us a note on the kitchen table. And do you know what's the worst part Frank? She's leaving when I'm graduating. One of the most important moments in my life, and she won't be here. That's so fucking wrong."

I told Celina that I was so sorry, and I held her in my arms. I then asked her if there was anything I could do. She replied, "Nah, Frank, you're doing enough. Thanks for just listening. It's just hard—you know? All this fucking talk about prom dresses, and I have no mom to help me find a dress and no money."

As I watched Celina cry for a second time, I told her, "Let me get you the prom dress. That's the least I can do."

Celina smiled through her tears and said, "Are you fucking serious? You want to buy me my prom dress? Do I get to pick it?"

August 1992 / Revere, Massachusetts

I watched Jessica as she chopped vegetables on the counter of her kitchen. She was wearing Daisy Duke denim shorts and a grey tank top with aqua lettering on the front that read, "Naughty Pussy." Jessica was a strident feminist, and during our mentor dinners at Pathways, she was always talking to our students about female empowerment.

I was confused because everything Jessica said and did was hypersexual, and this seemed contrary to female empowerment.

When I raised this contradiction with her, she replied, "It's a matter of taking back our power. When blacks started calling each other 'niggas' as a term of endearment, as a symbol of brotherhood, they were claiming something they had been called by the Klan and by all the other fucking racists in the world as their own.

"As women, we're doing the same thing: we're taking the language of our oppressor and turning it on its head. Men have been objectifying us for thousands of years. We're sex objects, playthings.

"You more than anyone should understand this. Wasn't the cross a humiliating way for Jesus to die? Christians then flipped it and made it into a symbol of hope and power."

Wow. I was impressed with Jessica's insight. We had been dating for three months, and she rarely pulled the veil back to give me an insight into why she said and did the things that she said and did. Not knowing the reason was unnerving, and I just defaulted to speculating.

I've realized that this was my critical mistake when it came to my relationships with women. Rather than asking questions, I would speculate or infer what women thought and felt through our interactions. On some level, I had been very unfair to Jessica.

For all Jessica's sexual bravado, she enjoyed playing around the edges of sexual intercourse. Or maybe she was continuing to expand my notion of what it meant to "have sex." I still wasn't ready to have sexual intercourse with Jessica. A part of me was still wrestling with the guilt of having left the seminary, and another part of me had built up my expectations about sex after all this time as a virgin.

I thought that being with the "right woman" was a prerequisite for having sex—especially for the first time. And I had my doubts about Jessica. There was something unbalanced about her that scared me, and it was difficult to imagine making a long-term commitment to her.

But the Hulk loved her. I wasn't sure whether this was love or lust. One time, after we had spent a day at the beach near her apartment, she went to the bathroom to take a shower. When Jessica entered the bedroom, she was naked, and she bent down to towel dry her hair. Seeing Jessica like this was incredibly erotic for me. It reminded me of the German university student whose ass I'd run into in Florence.

I kneeled down and started licking and biting Jessica's ass. As I was doing this, she said, "You're so fucking sexy. This is sexier than sex."

April 1993 / Chelsea, Massachusetts

A few hours before school started, I picked up Celina to go on the prom dress hunt. We went to several malls and department stores, but we weren't successful finding the right dress. One challenge was that Celina was six feet tall, and most stores didn't carry dresses in her size. We finally found a store that offered a good selection for tall women.

I sat on a red couch outside the dressing area, and Celina showed me a parade of dresses. They all looked incredible on her, but we hadn't yet found "the one." Celina really enjoyed trying on the dresses and at one point said to me, "Don't you feel like Richard Gere from *Pretty Woman*? I'm not saying that I see you that way. I mean, you're not my type. I'm just sayin' that this reminds me of the movie."

I concurred amusedly, and Celina continued to try on dresses.

Celina's Richard Gere comment was pretty representative of my interactions with female students. I was a young teacher, and they playfully flirted with me at times. Because I viewed them as kids, I didn't feel any sexual attraction even though they were beautiful in every way. My students trusted that I wouldn't do or say anything lecherous. In our advisories, we had heart-breaking moments when these young women shared their experiences of sexual abuse at the hands of the men who were supposed to protect them. As a teacher and as a man, I was committed to being a firewall of trust.

Within our staff planning sessions, we discussed our interactions with students. Building a culture of trust was a priority within Pathways, and this meant having courageous conversations about issues related to race, gender, and sexuality. Madison and Clare were white middle-class women, and Victor and I were Latinxs who came from working class families. Students tended to confide more often in me or Victor because our backgrounds were more similar to their own.

When Celina came out dressed in "the one," we celebrated our moment of triumph. The dress was a flowing but fitted gown that was white on top with detailed embroidery, and it had a neck strap that crisscrossed in the back and front. It then transitioned to black embroidery from the waist to the heels, with a stunning side slit that highlighted Celina's tall legs. I loved the contrast of colors between the gown and Celina's dark mocha skin. I stood there in awe, with the feelings that I imagined a father might have for his daughter.

Celina gave me a long hug and roared in triumph, "Frank, we fucking nailed this!"

After graduating from Pathways, Celina Lopes completed her undergraduate and graduate studies in education at the University of Massachusetts Boston. She became a celebrated teacher and administrator for the Boston Public Schools. Celina presently serves as the principal of a charter school in New Hampshire. She often cites the prom dress experience as a turning point in her life.

August 1992 / Revere, Massachusetts

Jessica was lying on top of me as she kissed me on the sand of Revere Beach. Being on top was her favorite position. Jessica always kissed me like she was kissing me for the last time. The feeling of finality made our kissing very intense and erotic.

She always smelled like the ocean when I came close to her, and I found this scent intoxicating. Jessica lived near the beach, and

I wondered if she spent a lot of time lying or walking on the beach—or maybe she was a mermaid. Even though I enjoyed my time with Jessica, I was wrestling with my feelings for her. I didn't know if I was experiencing love or simply lust.

I had delayed talking about my feelings with Jessica because I had such a sexual, primal attraction to her—the Hulk always responded to her call. While we were lying on Revere beach, I finally conjured the resolve to talk to her.

"Do you love me?" I asked.

"Before I answer your question, I need you to answer mine. Do you love me?" Jessica playfully asked.

I lay on the beach in silence and grasped at the sand.

Jessica did what she normally did and climbed on top of me. She had a look of concern as she looked down on me and said, "Fuck, this is not good. This is not good at all."

Jessica jumped to her feet and began running to the water. She then changed directions and ran parallel to the water. I stared at Jessica, and I felt a deep sadness for her and for us.

She eventually walked back to where I was lying, and she plopped herself next to me and said, "So, what do you want to do?"

I sat in silence for a few seconds and replied, "I think we know what we need to do."

She began to punch me as tears streamed from her eyes.

Jessica spoke through her tears, "You know, for a second, you made me believe that love was actually possible for me. And that's why I'm so fucking angry with you. Fuck, I should have trusted my first impression of you. I knew you were a fucking misogynst."

I had never asked Jessica why she thought I was misogynist. When she first announced this in the kitchen of Chelsea High School, I assumed she was upset that the students and I were operating from gender stereotypes: the female students were cooking and I was looking on. I knew that there was something deeper about her observation, but I never inquired about it.

Not asking was a mistake, but a part of me didn't want to know because I was afraid that there was a kernel of truth to it.

I got up and walked towards my car that was parked on the roadway adjacent to the beach and drove home. Jessica called me late the following night and rambled on incoherently. I wasn't sure if she was drunk, but I didn't understand a word she was saying. After warning her several times that I was going to hang up, I finally did.

I felt a twinge in my stomach when I hung up the phone. I would feel this twinge a number of times in the future. It was usually because I had serious doubts about whether I had done the right thing. Breaking up with Jessica was the first time that I had ever ended a relationship with a woman, and I didn't like the feeling. I didn't like the feeling of responsibility for slicing someone's heart. I felt the guilt of hurting her.

No one knew that I was still a virgin at the age of twenty-nine (with the exception of Jessica). This had become a monkey on my back. I realized that I had somehow associated sex with being damaged. I was born and raised in the United States, but because of my racial and ethnic background, I had internalized much of the cultures of Honduras and Italy. In those cultures, virginity is seen as the highest manifestation of the sacred. Girls who lose their virginity before marriage are considered "damaged goods." This standard doesn't apply to men—it's an unjust double standard that still exists today.

I had somehow flipped the standard and applied it to myself. In my mind, I could not fully embrace my divinity if I was "damaged" by sex. The gospels don't reveal the private life of Jesus. We don't know if he was ever married or had children. Because of the gospels' silence on the matter, the Catholic tradition advanced that he was celibate. On some psychological level, I was imitating the divinity of Jesus as modeled by him—or more accurately, as defined by Catholic tradition.

Because Jessica was so sexual, I saw her as damaged. I assumed that I could never be the person I wanted to be—fully divine and fully human—if I stayed with her. I feel a deep guilt; she deserved more. A big regret of mine is that I never gave Jessica more of a chance. I viewed her as a walking porn film, and she was so much more. The Hulk in me knew this truth, but Bruce Banner wanted to eradicate her from my life, just as he continually tried to eradicate the Hulk.

I didn't think that lust and love could coexist. I was operating from the misguided premise that being true to myself meant desexualizing spirituality.

The raging war within me would continue to devastate the lives of the women I loved. I was capable of so much damage because I was damaged.

GLORIOUS MYSTERY 4

COUPLES THERAPY

June 1994 / Manchester-by-the-Sea, Massachusetts

I popped open a bottle of chilled prosecco that I had taken from the cooler, and I poured it into two clear plastic cups. I handed one of the cups to Samantha, and she raised her cup for a toast:

"To the beginning of summer—may we enjoy many beautiful days," she said with a lilting British accent that made me feel like I was in a Shakespeare play.

As we sipped on our prosecco, I surveyed the beach. Singing Beach was one of my favorite locations for dates.

As I continued to look around, Samantha asked, "Are you ok? What are you looking at? If you're checking out other girls, I just wish you would be more discreet."

I laughed and replied, "No, I'm not checking out other girls, only the one in front of me."

Samantha flashed me a beautiful smile with her perfect teeth.

Samantha Taylor grew up in the Kensington section of London and carried herself with the grace of Audrey Hepburn. She was tall with tan skin and wore her short auburn hair, with its copper highlights, in a sideswept pixie cut. I had met her at a party in Brighton, and we discovered that we were both studying at Boston University (BU). She was getting her master's in music theory, and I had just begun a doctoral program in education. BU was offering scholarship opportunities to Chelsea teachers, and I was awarded a Title VII scholarship.

As I looked around the beach, my stomach churned to see a couple approaching us. As they were getting closer, I quietly said to myself, "Oh God."

A woman stood in front of us, stared at Samantha and said sternly, "What are you guys doing here? Samantha, why are you here with Frank? Where's Hilary?"

I stared at Monica, not knowing what to say. Monica was the younger sister of my girlfriend, Hilary Ryan, who I'd been dating for two years. I had forgotten that every Sunday of the summer, Monica and her boyfriend, Kyle, walked along Singing Beach. She had hosted the party in Brighton where Samantha and I had met. Hilary hadn't attended the party because she hadn't been feeling well.

Samantha stood up and protested, asking why it was a problem that we were at the beach together. She explained that we were on a date.

Monica replied in exasperation, "Samantha, Frank is my sister's boyfriend. They've been together for three years."

September 1994 / Chelsea, Massachusetts

The principal of Chelsea High School walked onto the stage of the auditorium and tapped on the microphone. Her name was Eva Hoffman and she had served as the principal of Chelsea High School for the past four years. She had convened a meeting of all teachers and staff to announce a major restructuring initiative at the high school. This would involve creating smaller learning communities for students. What this meant was that the high school would be divided into smaller schools, and each school would have a particular theme or focus.

This restructuring was in response to the passing of the Massachusetts Education Reform Act of 1993. This legislation instituted systemic changes: increased funding for K-12 schools, curriculum frameworks, and an accountability system (MCAS or the

Massachusetts Comprehensive Assessment System). The Reform Act also established charter schools and increased authority for principals and superintendents.

The other announcement was that a new high school would be built. The idea was to construct a new, innovative high school based upon the restructuring plan.

As principal Eva Hoffman spoke, I surveyed the room. A number of the teachers were smiling, others shaking their heads in disbelief. Richard Reynolds, a longtime English teacher, turned to me and said, "And this too shall pass."

Personally, I loved the new initiative. My experience at the Pathways School had taught me that we needed to completely rethink how we educated students, especially students of color.

After her presentation, the principal fielded questions, and then she invited individual teachers and staff to the stage to voice their reactions to the new initiative. Mario Ramos, a Puerto Rican teacher who worked in the ESL (English as a Second Language) department, approached the microphone to speak.

"I'm excited about this new direction that we're taking as a school," he said. "My students come from different cultures, from different languages. My students are suffering. They're suffering because they are being beaten down each day. They are being beaten down because of the color of their skin, the languages they speak, and the values of their families. We are failing them, and we have to stop."

As Mario was speaking, a chorus of loud boos began to echo through the auditorium.

Mario shouted over the boos, "The truth hurts! It's hard to hear that our staff is full of racists! But as the good book says, 'the truth will set you free!'"

I admired Mario's courage. And I agreed with him. He was one of the few Latinx teachers at Chelsea High School, which had an overwhelmingly white teaching staff.

My students at Pathways would routinely share horror stories about their experiences in traditional school. The challenges they faced were rooted in institutional racism. This was not the overt racism commonly associated with the Ku Klux Klan. It was racism that flowed from good intentions with little understanding of the power imbalances that were present in classrooms (white privilege). For example, Pathways students complained that white teaching staff at their previous schools focused on compliance and following rules—school felt like prison.

The proposed restructuring was about creating small learning communities to foster relationships among students and staff. Similar to Pathways, staff would have daily opportunities to know their students in a deeper way and to customize learning experiences to address their needs and interests.

After Mario spoke, a number of teachers vehemently denied Mario's indictment of the high school. They went onto the stage to defend the high school.

Janet Clark, a longtime math teacher, took the microphone and said, "Look, we're doing the best we can do given the circumstances. I am not and never have been a racist. I find Mr. Ramos' remarks very offensive. I've been teaching at this school for over twenty years, and I've seen a parade of dog and pony shows. One year we're doing this, and the next year we're doing that. I'm not against the restructuring plan. I'm just asking that we choose a plan and just stick with it. I love my kids, and I love my families. The real issue is poverty, and no one wants to talk about this. You're not going to do well if you're hungry or if you've been evicted from your apartment. I'm not a trained social worker, but I'm expected to be everything for these kids. And I feel completely overwhelmed. I don't get any support."

When I first heard Janet's comments, I was offended. I thought that she was throwing all the blame on students and their families and denying institutional racism.

Years later, I was more sympathetic to some of the import of her comments. Education reform over the last fifty years has operated from a well-intentioned but dangerous assumption: if we improve our educational system, we can fix the social inequities in our society. I believed this for years, and I was a champion for this belief. I've come to realize that comprehensive education reform will never change systemic inequities in our society. This is the root cause for why education reform has consistently failed.

June 1994 / Brighton, Massachusetts

During the drive back to her apartment in Brighton, Samantha refused to speak to me and exited my car without saying goodbye. She was upset that I hadn't told her about Hilary. I liked Samantha and she liked me. We had gone out on a few dates, but the guilt of cheating on Hilary had kept me from fully enjoying our time together.

However, I felt a strange apathy when she left the car. I recognized her simply as a player in my personal theatre. I felt a certain level of resignation that maybe love was not meant for me. I didn't want to believe it. But my heart feared this was the case, and it felt like howling wolves ready to devour hope.

When I arrived at my apartment, I took a beer from the fridge and monitored the phone. I was expecting a call from Hilary. I dreaded the call because I expected her pain and disappointment to compound the misery I was already experiencing in the relationship. I wanted out in the worst way.

A wave of hope washed across me when I realized that getting caught cheating on Hilary might become a blessing in disguise. I didn't have the courage to break up with Hilary, but I had unintentionally set up a two-act improv play. Act 1: I cheat on Hilary with Samantha. Act 2: Monica reports my indiscretion to her sister, Hilary. She becomes furious and then, voilà, Hilary breaks up with me and demands never to see me again.

As I sipped on my beer, I realized that I had stumbled onto an exit plan.

When the phone rang, I waited three rings before I answered the phone. Hilary was on the other line.

"Frank, I just talked to Monica. Is it true? Are you screwin' around?"

"It was only one date," I lied. "I met her at Monica's party," I said nervously.

"What were you thinking? We've invested so much in this relationship, and you're ready to toss it all away?" Hilary paused and then asked, "Do you love her?"

"No, I don't love her. I barely know her." I replied.

"Ok, just make sure it never happens again," Hilary said firmly.

"So you want to stay together?" I asked incredulously.

"I'm not throwing it all away. All couples go through this. We can get through this," Hilary explained.

After I had hung up the receiver, I sprawled upon my apartment sofa and lay there in crushing silence. I couldn't believe that the second act of my play turned out to have an unexpected twist.

The phone conversation was so reflective of our relationship. Hilary tended to think and act for the two of us. She rarely asked what I wanted or what I thought about things. Hilary felt comfortable taking charge of any situation and just moving forward. Just move forward. This was Hilary's approach to life.

I had met Hilary Ryan in high school. We had graduated at the top of our class at Stoneham High School. Hilary went to Dartmouth College, while I had left for Saint John's Seminary College. We weren't really friends in high school, but we respected each other's commitment to academics in a school and town that was anti-intellectual and primarily concerned with the weekly high school sports drama, straight out of *Friday Night Lights*.

Hilary was the embodiment of Sandy Olsson, Olivia Newton John's character in the movie musical *Grease*. She was the all-American girl, and I was both attracted to and repulsed by her. The repulsion was not her fault. Her popularity in high school reminded me that I wasn't the all-American boy—I didn't look or act the part. I was an outsider.

We had reconnected a couple months after I had broken up with Jessica. I had gone to mass with my mom at Saint Patrick's Church, my home parish in Stoneham. Hilary had come with her parents, who were very active in the parish. Hilary looked really good when I saw her, and she seemed to have a new interest in me. Somehow I had become Danny Zuko, John Travolta's carefree rebel character.

I had originally welcomed dating Hilary because she was so different from Jessica. She was modest. She was humble. She rarely swore. And she had gone to Dartmouth College. Hilary was the woman that every mom would want her son to marry.

Within a few weeks of dating Hilary, I had confided in her that I was still a virgin. She was surprised, but she didn't think it was strange. She knew that I had spent six years in the seminary. I sensed that she welcomed the idea that making love to her would be my first experience. Hilary found it very romantic.

I lost my virginity to Hilary shortly before my thirtieth birthday. The experience was not what I had hoped for. She lived in an apartment in Maynard and she had a waterbed. When I had finally decided to take the plunge into sex, I didn't know that the experience would be literal. I was swimming around in the waterbed as we awkwardly engaged in our attempt at lovemaking. Maybe that was the issue: I wanted it to be lovemaking, but I didn't love Hilary. The other challenge was that I still felt emotionally conflicted. Hilary hugged me after we finished, and while it wasn't as enjoyable as I had wanted it to be, the monkey was finally off my back.

October 1993 / Cambridge, Massachusetts

Our students were standing in a circle as Cheryl Chambers, the director of the Roxbury Shakespeare Company, led us in a breathing exercise.

"You need to breathe from your diaphragm, or you won't be able to finish your lines—you'll be out of breath."

Cheryl was a Black woman in her sixties who had grown up in Roxbury. She had spent years as an actor in several theatre groups, and she had made a life-changing decision to bring Shakespeare to the children of Boston.

The Roxbury Shakespeare Company was based out of the Massachusetts Institute of Technology (MIT). Pathways had partnered with her company as part of our Shakespeare project. The purpose was not only to expose students to Shakespeare but also to build their skill and confidence in public speaking. As we were doing the breathing exercise, Danny Sok, a student from Cambodia, began to complain about doing the exercises.

"You're afraid, Danny. I can see that. I want you to push through your fear," Cheryl said assertively.

"I'm not afraid of nothing, Miss. This is just fucking boring."

She studied Danny for a few seconds and said, "I want you to say as loud as you can without screaming, 'This is just fucking boring.' But remember to use your diaphragm."

Danny began to laugh and yelled, "This is just fucking boring!"

"Danny, you're yelling and not speaking, and you're not using your diaphragm. Do it again." said Cheryl.

He nervously adjusted his jacket, looked around the room, and then firmly said in a deep voice, "This is just fucking boring."

Cheryl applauded and said, "Can you hear the difference? A moment ago you sounded like a whiny child and now you're sounding like a king."

Danny took off his hat, rubbed his head, and beamed a beautiful smile.

July 1994 / Concord, Massachusetts

Shortly after our phone call, Hilary had given me an ultimatum about getting engaged. She told me that I had two months, or it was over. Hilary had also insisted that we begin couples counseling immediately, and she had already scheduled our first meeting with a therapist based out of Concord.

I was thinking of waiting out the two months, but I was afraid that she would find a way to keep us together. I had dinner at my mom's house to explain my predicament and told her about my indiscretion.

"Honey, how could you do that to Hilary? She's always been very sweet to you. And I feel sorry for the other poor girl. If you don't want to be with Hilary, why don't you just break up with her?" my mom inquired.

"Mom, I don't know. Breaking up with her feels like breaking up with the Virgin Mary. And now she wants me to go to couples counseling."

"So what do you plan to do?" my mother asked.

"Could you call her and break up with her for me?" I implored. "I know that sounds ridiculous, but I'm desperate."

My mother began to laugh and said, "Francis, you're a grown man. You have to do this. You have to clean up your own mess. I'm not going to clean up after you."

"It's just that I need someone, a third party, who could hold me responsible for what I'm saying when I'm breaking up with her. Someone to keep me from folding. Even if it was just a little dog—that could do it."

"Well, if you're going to a couples counselor, why don't you tell the counselor? The counselor can hold you accountable."

When my mother made this suggestion, I jumped from the kitchen chair and kissed her.

I had asked Hilary to meet me at the therapist's house because I was hoping and praying that once our relationship was over, we would need to drive separate cars. I arrived at the session first, and a middle-aged woman, shaped like an apple, invited me into her home. She was using a section of her first floor to see clients, and French doors separated her practice from the rest of the house.

Hilary arrived wearing the army green Chico's dress that I had given her for her birthday. She sat next to me on the couch and took my hand.

As the therapist was giving an overview of her approach to therapy, I interrupted her and said, "Before we get any deeper into this. I just want to be clear that this is my first and last session. My intention is to break up with Hilary."

Hilary studied me with a look of shock and said, "Frank, you're breaking up with me?"

The therapist got up from her chair and said, "The two of you may want to take a two-week break before we start our first session."

"There won't be any two-week break. It's over," I asserted.

The therapist then asked to speak with me alone, inviting Hilary to leave the room.

"Frank, what's happening?" she asked. "Hilary obviously had no idea that you wanted to break up with her. Why did you agree to couples therapy?"

"I never agreed to couples therapy. She announced that we were doing it, and she gave me an ultimatum that unless we got engaged in two months, our relationship would be over. I've wasted three years of my life, and I don't want to waste a day more."

"How do you feel about Hilary?" asked the therapist.

"To be honest, I feel nothing. I never loved her. I think she knows this, but for some reason, she wants this charade to continue. The only thing I feel is anger—anger at myself for allowing this to go on for so long."

The therapist got up from her chair, opened the French doors, and invited Hilary to join us. After Hilary sat down, the therapist turned to me and said, "Frank, I want you to repeat to Hilary exactly what you told me, word for word."

I squirmed in my chair for a few seconds, and then I told Hilary what I'd said to the therapist.

Hilary rose from her seat and, through her tears, screamed like a banshee, "Get the fuck out! Get the fuck out! Get the fuck out!" She then turned away from me and began shaking.

I left the therapist's home and got into my car. As I was turning the ignition, I noticed that the therapist had a very large gravel driveway, and I began to rev up the engine. My car had a standard clutch, and when I put it into first gear, I did a doughnut out of her driveway. As I sped along Route 2 towards Cambridge, I started blasting AC/DC's anthem "Highway to Hell" on my car stereo. I felt the adrenaline coursing through my body as I listened to the lyrics, "No stop signs, speed limit. Nobody's gonna slow me down."

I was free. I was finally free.

I hadn't seen Hilary for twenty-five years until, when her father died in 2019, she invited me to the wake and funeral. Her father and mother had always been very kind to me and my family. Although seeing Hilary with her husband and beautiful family did soothe the sting a bit, when I hugged her in the family reception line at the wake, I felt a deep regret for hurting her. The bottom line is that I had been dishonest with her for the whole time we were dating—since day one. I had accused her of orchestrating the charade that we were actually a couple, but I was really the one who was the primary architect.

Because of my inner conflict, I had chosen to date Hilary because she was the opposite of Jessica. Hilary was the Virgin Mary. I felt comfortable dating her because I believed I could become the person I had wanted to become—fully divine and fully human. The problem was that I had placed Jessica and Hilary at opposite ends of the spectrum: Jessica was the whore, and Hilary was the Virgin Mary. My love was dualistic: the Hulk loved Jessica, and Dr. Bruce Banner loved Hilary.

I've had an epiphany about the true nature of love. I realized that I had bought into the greatest lie ever told—romantic love. Even though we live in a modern world, we still embrace an understanding of romantic love from the eleventh century, the days of knights and courtesans.

This understanding of love is the source of our deepest illusions, and it's the destroyer of relationships. It's a love that resists everything that is moldy, mossy, and messy. It prefers the smooth over the granular, clear skies over misty rain.

I'm not saying that romance is the problem. Romance is beautiful and can nurture a relationship. But there is a difference between romance and romantic love. The former can lead to a deeper love, but the latter is as delicate as butterfly wings and will disintegrate with one touch of the real.

234 LAKEVIEW

September 1996 / Chelsea, Massachusetts

Wade stared into home plate and then looked over at first base where our student Yolanda Rivas was dancing on and off the base, daring Wade to throw in her direction. Wade Evans, a computer teacher, went into his windup and twisted his torso like Red Sox pitching legend Luis Tiant as he threw a high arching pitch towards home plate. Cindy Strom, an English teacher, was in the batter's box and patiently waited for the ball. She lifted her front leg as she swung at the pitch and sent the ball careening over the shortstop for a base hit. Yolanda was clapping at second base and cheered Cindy as she arrived at first base. Cindy pointed at Yolanda and jumped up and down on first base in celebration.

It was a perfect fall day, and the staff and students of the Bridge School were playing softball in the large parking lot of the old Chelsea Armory. The Bridge School was a new small school that had been created under the Chelsea High School restructuring plan. The school was modeled after the Pathways School, but it ran during the regular school hours of 8:00 a.m. to 2:30 p.m. Because of my doctoral study commitments, I had decided to transfer to the Bridge School. I was very happy to learn that Madison, Clare, and Victor were transfering there, too. They were parents of young children and the evening hours at Pathways were becoming increasingly difficult. A new wave of young teachers would now run the Pathways School.

Chelsea High School opened in September of 1996 with four new schools within a school: the Bridge School, the Classical Arts School, the Commerce and Communications School, and the International School. Each school had a theme and focus of study, and students and families had chosen their respective school the previous spring. There were approximately 250 students that attended each school. It was an exciting time in Chelsea because staff and students had an opportunity to participate in an education revolution. The opening of the schools mirrored the opening of a baseball season—it was full hope.

August 1996 / Cambridge, Massachusetts

I struck a wooden match and lit up a chocolate-colored torpedo cigar on the back porch of my apartment. John O'Brien, my upstairs neighbor and a Chelsea High School colleague, had traveled to Italy with his wife, Rosa, and they brought me back a box of Romeo y Julieta cigars and port wine. It was a very generous gift, and as I puffed on my cigar and tasted the sweetness of the port, I thought how blessed I was to live at 234 Lakeview Avenue in Cambridge, Massachusetts.

The house is a mile and a half from Harvard Square, in northwest Cambridge. The three-story, Federal-style wood frame building was constructed in 1796 by Jacob Wyeth, a graduate of nearby Harvard College. The building served as a resort hotel, because it bordered Fresh Pond. The hotel was briefly converted into a convent in 1886. And in 1892, it was moved to its present location at 234 Lakeview.

I had moved to 234 Lakeview in 1992, a few months after I started working in Chelsea. I was fortunate—because of rent control, I was able to rent an affordable apartment in Cambridge. This was an exciting time to live in Cambridge because of the racial, cultural, and ethnic diversity. Unfortunately, rent control was later lifted through a statewide referendum in 1995, and this has contributed to the inceasing economic stratification in Cambridge that still exists today.

The building now served as an apartment building with eight units. It was occupied by a concert pianist, a clown/magician, an environmental planner, an MBA student, a nurse, a paralegal, a couple of public school teachers (including me), and a social worker. Before the show *Friends* existed, we had 234 Lakeview. I had missed my community at the seminary, and 234 Lakeview provided me with a new and vibrant community.

November 1996 / Chelsea, Massachusetts

The educational and social experiment that was Chelsea High School had a promising beginning, but the afterglow was beginning to wane. One of the key challenges was that although the school was now reorganized into four different schools, the mindsets of staff were still the same in the development and execution of curricula.

At the Bridge School, we had a history teacher who was very committed to social justice, and we were excited to have a progressive educator on our staff. His name was Jacob Levy, and he was a kind and compassionate soul. The problem was that he had a very traditional approach to his classroom: he relied primarily upon lectures and having students answer questions at the end of assigned readings. Jacob had not fully embraced project-based learning, and the idea of the teacher as a facilitator of learning—rather than as an expert—challenged his professional identity.

Another challenge was that a number of our students required specific learning interventions. Our student demographic included English learners and students with disabilities. At the Pathways School, we had believed that all teachers were responsible for every aspect of a student's educational program. At the Bridge School, some teachers did not share this approach and tended to operate within the parameters of their professional credentials. They believed that special education teachers were exclusively responsible for students with disabilities, and ESL (English as a Second Language) teachers were exclusively responsible for English learners.

As the school year progressed, I started taking on more responsibility for working with students with disabilities because some of my colleagues felt it wasn't their responsibility. This was a tension that was not only operative within the Bridge School but across all the school programs at Chelsea High School.

September 1996 / Cambridge, Massachusetts

As I was smoking my cigar on the back porch, Milena came outside to join me. She slowly sat on my lap, sipped on my glass of port, and took a puff from my cigar. Milena was about to begin her final year at Wellesley College where she was majoring in psychology. She also worked part-time as an office administrator for a cardiologist at Mount Auburn Hospital in Cambridge.

In March of 1993, she had responded to an ad for a roommate that I had posted. I had over forty respondents to the ad and spent two weeks interviewing people. During the interviews, I asked mostly lifestyle questions: What's your work or school schedule? Do you like to have people over? What's your approach to sharing expenses? Not only was I looking for shared values around lifestyle, but I was looking for someone who was friendly, communicative, and just a decent human being.

At the time, I was still seeing Hilary, and she was hoping that I would choose a male roommate. Most of the men I interviewed had a frat boy quality that I couldn't imagine living with. While the women interviewed better than the men, a number of them were very attractive, and I knew that Hilary wouldn't approve.

I decided on Milena because I felt comfortable with her, and I was convinced that I would never be tempted to get involved with her. I have no clue why I believed this. Milena Janssen was a strikingly beautiful woman. She was tall—five foot ten—with an athletic and voluptuous build, long chestnut colored hair, and large and penetrating brown eyes. She looked and talked like the actress Geena Davis. Milena moved into my apartment in April of 1993.

At the beginning, Hilary felt a little threatened by Milena, but after a few months, she realized that I only saw Milena as a roommate and friend. Milena had a number of suitors, and there seemed to be no rhyme or reason to her dating choices. She dated blue collar guys, white collar guys, tall, short, handsome, ugly, intelligent, stupid. Milena was twenty-five, and she had once dated a helicopter pilot almost twice her age who had worked on the movie *Jurassic Park*.

Milena had more than a few one-night stands. Her dates were a little embarrassed when our paths crossed in the kitchen, but I tried to ease the awkwardness by inviting them for breakfast. And for the most part, I enjoyed talking with them. After they left, she would debrief me about what had happened, and I found her stories very entertaining.

We became close friends, and we enjoyed being witnesses to each other's lives. Milena helped me through my breakup with Hilary, and she coached me through my dating life that included a flamenco dancer, a doctoral student in philosophy, a high school biology teacher, and a journalist.

It was August of 1996 when we decided to take a trip to Greece. My classmate from Boston University was from Greece, and she had invited me and Milena to stay at her family's home in Athens. After a few days in Athens, we traveled to the islands of Mykonos and Paros. Greek men loved Milena, and she relied on me to protect her because they could be aggressive. Milena was tough, and she could smack down any guy at any time, but there were instances when a group of Greek men would converge on her, and I would help her to slip away. When we returned home from Greece, everything changed.

April 1997 / Boston, Massachusetts

Penelope Díaz rummaged through the papers in her folder and found the document she was looking for. She whispered to José Alcantara, who was about to cross-examine a witness. José asked the judge if he could confer for a couple of minutes with his legal team.

Jackie Schneider and I were sitting in the audience, wondering what our students were discussing. We were the advisors for the Bridge School team that was participating in the Mock Trial Competition sponsored by the Massachusetts Bar Association.

The purpose of the program was to provide opportunities for high school students to hone their skills as lawyers and witnesses in a simulated courtroom setting, where they would learn the fundamentals of the American judicial system. High schools competed against each other, and the presiding judge decided which team had argued its case most effectively. The Bridge School was competing against the Boston Latin School, an elite school within the Boston Public Schools. Students who attended Boston Latin had to score high in an entrance exam. We were the underdogs entering the competition.

Jackie had been a lawyer before she taught at the Bridge School. She was serving as the school-to-work coordinator and was responsible for overseeing the student internship program. Students did internships in Boston, Chelsea, and Cambridge, and the internships spanned across sectors: health, science, legal, political, education, and financial. I was learning Massachusetts law along with the students, but I knew I had the potential to be a great lawyer—I had never lost a case involving parking tickets. Jackie and I worked well together, and we coached the Bridge School team to prepare their case for the mock trial competition.

The judge asked if the Chelsea legal team was ready. Penelope approached the witness bench and said, "Mr. Curtis, you testified before this court that you saw the defendant run out of the convenience store at 9:30 p.m. but, in your affidavit, you stated that he left the store at 8:00 p.m. Which was it?" One of the students on the Boston Latin team slammed his fist on the table; their team had muffed the witness testimony during the court proceeding. The judge looked over at Penelope and smiled. She did a quick fist pump and continued her cross-examination.

August 1996 / Cambridge, Massachusetts

Milena and I were having a beer in the kitchen. We were tired from the long flight back from Greece. She was a connoisseur of microbrews and had sharpened my beer palate with her selections.

As she sipped a bottle of apricot-flavored beer, Milena nervously said, "Frank, believe it or not, I think I have feelings for you. I've had them for some time, but I just thought that you didn't see me in that way."

I sat in silence for a few seconds, a little surprised by her admission. "I didn't think you saw *me* in that way. We've been living together for almost three years, and I didn't have an inkling that you felt this way," I replied.

Milena looked at me intensely and said with frustration, "Fuck, don't leave me hangin'. How do you see me?"

I smiled and said, "I was in love with you the first time I saw you."

She laughed and said, "You are so full of shit. Please just be serious for a moment." Tears were forming in her eyes as she waited for my response.

"Milena, I've always liked you. And yeah, at some point, I started feeling something more than friendship." She was standing by the stove. I walked over to her and kissed her.

After we kissed, she invited me to her bedroom. She laughed and asked if we were going too fast since we were finally going to have sex after three years of knowing each other. She told me to take off my clothes and to keep my eyes closed as I waited on her bed. I promised her, on my father's grave, not to open my eyes.

She left the room for a few minutes, and when she came back, I heard the click of a cassette player opening and closing. When she played the tape, the theme from the 1970s TV show *Wonder Woman* was playing. I began to laugh and asked if I could open my eyes.

She replied, "No! Keep your freakin' eyes closed. I'll tell you when to open them." A few seconds later she announced boldly, "My name is Diana, princess of Themyscira and daughter to Queen Hippolyta. You know me as Wonder Woman. Ok, open your eyes."

When I opened my eyes, Milena was wearing a revealing red bra and blue panties. She stood there smiling in Wonder Woman's power position, with her hands on her hips. I thought to myself, "Wow. Goodbye Aphrodite. And hello Wonder Woman."

I began to laugh and asked, "How did you know about my thing for Wonder Woman?"

Milena climbed on top of me and said, "I've known about your Wonder Woman fetish for three years. You watch her fucking show almost every day. By the way, my tits are bigger than Lynda Carter's. She has a C cup and mine are double D."

From that day forward, I became well versed in women's bra cup, panty, and dress sizes. I became a regular at Victoria's Secret.

We made love on Milena's bed, and I enjoyed it immensely. I had a chemistry with her that I hadn't experienced since Jessica. The difference was that Milena didn't have to operate around my boundaries. She could run free. And man, could she run.

After my first sexual encounter with Hilary, my feelings of guilt and angst associated with sex had waned. I had sex regularly with the women I dated after Hilary, and with each experience, I felt more confident. I learned that sex was as natural as breathing, and the Hulk within me felt vindicated.

However, it did feel different with Milena. I loved her. And this is what I had hoped lovemaking would look, sound, and feel like.

This was the first time that I saw the sacred within the act of sex. For most of my adult life, I had desexualized spirituality. I thought that God could only be known through a denial of the physical. I came to a deeper realization: that the spiritual could only be experienced through the physical. I now understood the powerful insight by Jesuit priest, philosopher, and paleontologist Pierre Teilhard de Chardin: "We are not human beings having a spiritual experience. We are spiritual beings having a human experience."

April 1997 / Boston, Massachusetts

We waited for the judge's decision, and I looked over at the students. José was drawing a courtroom sketch of me and held it up proudly for me to see—I looked like Frankenstein. He started laughing at my less-than-amused reaction.

Jackie put her arms around me and said, "Frank, I just wanted you to know that regardless of what happens, I'm really proud of the kids, and I'm proud of the work we did together. You're so good at what you do, and you make it so much fun. And this year..." Jackie's voice trailed off, and she began choking up. She continued, "And this year, both personally and professionally, has been the best year of my life. I really needed this."

When I looked over at the students, they were concerned that Jackie was crying. I waved them off and mouthed silently that she was ok. Jackie began to quietly laugh and told me that she had never cried in a courtroom.

I wrapped my arm around her shoulder and said, "The feeling is completely mutual, counselor. We never, ever could have pulled this off without you. Counselor, I just have one fundamental disagreement with you—fuck moral victories. Just win, baby. Just win."

Jackie broke into tears of laughter because she was a huge NFL football fan. She was well versed in the sayings of Al Davis, former owner of the Oakland (now Las Vegas) Raiders.

The judge returned to her bench and said, "I want to congratulate both teams for your performance today. Your hard work and preparation were on full display. You should be proud of what you accomplished. I believe both teams deserve to win today's competition, but I can choose only one. The winner of today's Mock Trial competition is Chelsea High School."

An explosion of cheers and moans detonated in the courtroom. Our Chelsea students were throwing their courtroom papers in the air like confetti. I hugged Jackie and yelled, "That's what I'm talking about, baby!" I walked over to the students to congratulate them, and they began a mock chant of "Jim-my, Jim-my, Jim-my!" because they had this long-standing joke that I looked like the actor Jimmy Smits from the TV show *LA Law*.

I went over to shake the hands of the teacher advisors for the Boston Latin team. I felt sorry for them because I knew the pain of losing. Losing was my best friend. When Jackie told me that I was good at what I did, I balked at her compliment. In my head and heart, I was a failure 90 percent of the time with my students, and 10 percent of the time I succeeded. Today was a great 10 percent day.

September 1996 / Cambridge, Massachusetts

As Milena was sitting on my lap and puffing on my cigar on the back porch, she asked me if we could continue the interview we had started for her independent study. She was doing a research project studying the psychosocial development of males, and she was using Erik Erikson's eight stages of psychosocial development as the framework for her research. In addition to interviewing me, she was also interviewing two other residents of 234 Lakeview: John O'Brien, a colleague from Chelsea High School, and Randy Simmons, who was a professional clown and magician. Milena went inside the apartment and came out with her notebook. She sat across from me and put on her glasses. I smiled as I was studying her. She had her long hair pulled back in a ponytail, and she shifted into her professional Wellesley College student mode. There was something incredibly sexy about it.

I asked, "Are you Diana Prince now? Isn't it a little dangerous that I know your secret identity?"

She laughed and replied, "Don't get used to the Wonder Woman shit. That bra strap was killing me. My girls were suffocating. I do want to know more about your other sexual fantasies and fetishes. I've already pieced some of them together, and I've started connecting the dots."

I was a little nervous that Milena was so sure of herself, and I asked what she had "pieced together."

"Do you really want to hear this? Can you handle the truth?" She said mockingly, imitating Jack Nicholson's character from *A Few Good Men*. Milena continued, "Ok, I'm going to go light and then get to the meatier stuff. In addition to the Wonder Woman fetish, you have a female foot and shoe fetish. You also have a thing for women's body scent. They're probably connected."

"Whaaat? You call this going light? What are you basing this on?"

She jumped out of her seat and quickly entered the apartment. When she came back, she plopped her black high heels on my lap, and said, "This is exhibit A."

I sat there stunned and embarrassed.

She continued, "Did you really think that I hadn't noticed that you were doing something with my heels? My hunch is that you were smelling them."

We shared a common walk-in closet, and shortly before our trip to Greece, I would periodically pick up her heels that were on a hanging shoe rack and sniff them. I was just devastated that she knew this. I was really embarrassed, and I was looking down at the floorboards of the porch deck as I smoked my cigar.

She came over, knelt in front of me and said, "Frank, it's ok. It's natural. We all have some kind of sexual fetish or fantasy. It's a part of who we are." She continued, "If you don't mind me going a little further, exhibit B happened last night."

I was anxiously curious and asked, "What is exhibit B?"

She stood up, flashed a beautiful smile, and explained, "Exhibit B happened while we were doing it. I noticed that you were poking your nose around on me like an animal. You were smelling me and to be honest, I was getting off on it. You had an animal quality when we were doing it. And I liked it. I liked it a lot. Are you ready for exhibit C?"

"Oh god. What is exhibit C?" I asked reluctantly.

"After we had fallen asleep, you went to the bathroom in the middle of the night. When you came back, you thought I was still asleep, but I wasn't. You started sniffing my feet, and then my legs, and then my ass, and then my back, and then the pits of my arms, and then my neck, and then my hair. I loved it. I absolutely fucking loved it. I didn't say anything last night because I didn't want to embarrass you."

I sat in silence as I sipped on my port, savoring its sweetness and Milena Janssen's stunning discoveries. She was serving as the ultimate mirror to my human desires. And she was mirroring them without judgment and without shame. She was mirroring love.

LUMINOUS
MYSTERIES

Your defects are the ways that glory gets manifested ...
That's where the Light enters you.

~ Rumi

COFFEE SHOP
CONFESSION

October 1996 / Chelsea, Massachusetts

It was Halloween, and I ran into Dunkin' Donuts in Chelsea Square for my daily morning cup of joe. I was running a little late on my way to Chelsea High School, and I was hoping that the line wouldn't be too long. As I entered, an elderly woman greeted me with a warm smile and she blessed herself as she left the coffee shop. I was wondering why she had blessed herself when she passed me, but I was preoccupied with getting to school on time.

As I waited in line, I heard sniffling behind me. The sniffling then turned into a quiet moan. When I turned around, a thirtyish-year-old man, small in stature with a weathered face, looked up at me with tears in his eyes.

I asked him if he was all right and he replied, *"Buenos días, Padre. Lamento molestarlo, pero es un milagro que esté parado frente a mí"* "Good morning, Father. I'm sorry to bother you, but it's a miracle that you're standing in front of me."

I was wondering why he was addressing me as "Father," and then I abruptly realized why: I was dressed in my priest clerics.

Before I could explain, he asked, *"Padre, ¿podrías escuchar mi confesión?"* "Father, could you hear my confession?"

"Oh God," I thought to myself. How could I have forgotten that I was dressed in clerics? Every Halloween, I had a tradition of wearing my priest clerics to Chelsea High School. My students were fascinated with my previous life as a priest-in-training. Students and teachers loved to dress in an array of creative costumes, and I had decided to wear "the suit." The students loved it, and they would ask me to perform mock exorcisms where I would recite the famous line, "The power of Christ compels you!" from the cult horror movie *The Exorcist*.

Before I could explain to the man that I was wearing a Halloween costume, he began to sob and said, *"Le pedí a Dios una señal esta mañana y aquí está usted. ¡Esto es un milagro!"* "I had asked God for a sign this morning and here you are. This is a miracle!"

When we arrived at the front of the line, a young female server said, "Wow, I never knew you were a priest. I thought you worked at the high school?" I was hoping that the man behind me had heard the server, but he didn't. Or maybe he didn't understand her.

"The usual, right? Large coffee with one cream and one sugar?" the server asked.

The man stepped in front of me and gave the server a ten dollar bill, telling her that he was paying for me. I tried to stop him, but he insisted and then ordered a small coffee and a blueberry muffin. He surveyed the coffee shop and directed me to a corner.

As I was building my resolve to tell him the truth, he said, *"Padre, he lastimado a mi familia de muchas maneras. Necesito hacer las cosas bien."* "Father, I've hurt my family in so many ways. I need to make things right." Through his tears, he began his confession.

January 1997 / Cambridge, Massachusetts

Milena opened the oven door, and I placed a large pan of jambalaya inside. We were hosting a Super Bowl party—the Patriots were playing the Green Bay Packers. It was their first Super Bowl appearance in a decade, since their embarrassing loss and complete destruction (46–10) at the hands of the Chicago Bears.

Because the game was being played in New Orleans, I decided to do a Creole homage and made jambalaya. As Milena was cutting up a French baguette, I could smell the oven simmering with chorizo, garlic, marinated chicken, mussels, shrimp, onions, peppers, tomatoes, black beans, and olive oil. She offered me a beer, and we clicked our bottles for a quick toast. Milena seemed a little distracted, but because the game was about to begin, I was focused on setting up for the party.

Most of our 234 Lakeview neighbors joined us: Sabrina and Sachi, sisters studying for their MBAs who were an interesting ethnic mix of Egyptian and Swedish; Amazing Randy, our resident clown/magician, and his girlfriend, Carmen, a pediatric nurse; Maureen, a social worker, and her boyfriend, Sam, a college professor; my Chelsea colleague John O'Brien and his wife, Rosa, a high school math teacher.

As most of the country and planet knows, Boston sports fans are fiercely fanatical. We were yelling and screaming at the TV as if Patriots' coach Bill Parcells and quarterback Drew Bledsoe were sitting across from us in the living room. We were deflated when the Patriots, yet again, found a way to lose to Brett Favre and the Green Bay Packers, 35–21. This was the era before the Golden Age of Bill Belichick and Tom Brady.

After we finished the post-party clean up, Milena and I sat on the sofa and watched the news. She playfully pointed her bare feet at my face, and I pretended not to notice. I was still smarting from the Super Bowl loss. Milena then got up and stormed out of the living room. I didn't follow her.

October 1996 / Chelsea, Massachusetts

The coffee shop confessor was a recent immigrant from Colombia. He had two wives and two families—one set in Colombia and one in Chelsea. What weighed on him was not what he was doing but what he wasn't doing. He felt like an inadequate husband and father to both families.

What I remembered most about his confession was his breathing. At the beginning, his breathing was labored and he was barely able to speak. Towards the end of his confession, his breathing was light and his voice sounded more animated. He asked me if he was going to go to hell.

I told him, "No, God doesn't operate that way. We're the ones who choose heaven or hell in this life or the next."

We agreed that he would speak to both his wives and share the truth about his double life. Regardless of the fallout, he would be committed to taking care of the people he loved. For penance, I told him to pray one Our Father and three Hail Marys. I placed my hands on his head and felt inspired to do the prayer of absolution in Latin:

> *Deus, Pater misericordiárum, qui per mortem et resurrectiónem Fílii sui mundum sibi reconciliávit et Spíritum Sanctum effúdit in remissiónem peccatórum, per ministérium Ecclésiæ indulgéntiam tibi tríbuat et pacem. Et ego te absólvo a peccátis tuis in nómine Patris, et Fílii, et Spíritus Sancti. Amen.*

> God, the Father of mercies, through the death and resurrection of His Son has reconciled the world to Himself and sent the Holy Spirit among us for the forgiveness of sins; through the ministry of the Church may God give you pardon and peace, and I absolve you from your sins in the name of the Father, and of the Son, and of the Holy Spirit. Amen.

His head was still bowed. I placed my hands on his shoulders and said, *"Hermano, vas a estar bien."* "Brother, you're going to be ok."

I hugged him, and I could feel his tears dropping on my shoulders—I was grateful that they were tears of joy. We then fell into a fit of laughter when a slightly intoxicated, middle-aged woman complained loudly in a very thick Boston accent, "What the fuck? A priest is listening to confessions in a fucking Dunkin' Donuts?"

I wasn't fully present when I arrived at Chelsea High School. I was still thinking about my coffee shop confession. I was wondering whether my Colombian friend would be ok.

January 1997 / Cambridge, Massachusetts

When I entered the bedroom, Milena was propped up on a pillow reading a book.

She didn't look at me when I came in, and as I took off my clothes, she calmly asked me, "Do you know how many times you called Drew Bledsoe a fucking idiot during the game?"

"I have no idea. Maybe ten times?" I replied.

"No, not even close. Thirty-seven times. I counted. And I thought it was very ironic," Milena emphatically stated.

"What's so ironic? That I was stating the obvious?" I asked.

"Stating the obvious is not irony."

Milena then hopped off the bed and grabbed the dictionary from her desk and read out loud, "'Irony: the use of words to express something other than and especially the opposite of the literal meaning.' It also means 'the incongruity between the actual result of a sequence of events and the normal or expected result.' Ergo, stating the obvious is not irony."

"Thank you, Dr. Janssen, for a brilliant explanation. And may I ask the point?" I inquired sarcastically.

"You accused Drew Bledsoe of being a fucking idiot because of the lost opportunities that he left on the field. And you were right—he was a fucking idiot because he played like shit. But you, Dr. DeVito— you are guilty of the same crime. Lost opportunities."

"What do you mean 'lost opportunities'? Just because I didn't accept your not-so-subtle invitation? We just lost the fucking Super Bowl, and I'm supposed to get it on with you right after the game?" I defensively replied.

"That's my whole fucking point. You're always waiting for the 'right opportunity,' and when it's knocking on your door, your response is 'Sorry, it's not the right time.' When is the right fucking time? And why do you get to decide?" Milena said defiantly.

She continued, "I'm going to tell you something that you won't want to hear. I feel alone most of the time when I'm with you. You are somewhere else, and I have no fucking idea how to reach you. Offering you sex is the only incentive I've got and even that doesn't work."

She lay down in bed, pulling the covers over her head.

Milena's indictment stung, and I didn't disagree with her. I just didn't know how to change.

My dilemma reminded me of a key finding in Milena's independent study about the psychosocial development of males. According to Erikson's developmental framework, I was in stage 6: intimacy vs. isolation. His thesis was that our ability to develop meaningful and healthy relationships with others was based upon a strong sense of self. Milena noted in the case study of me that I had struggled to develop this sense of self, and my tendency was to isolate myself rather than allow myself to be vulnerable.

I agreed with her assessment that I struggled with intimacy with women and others. I had made a positive shift with regard to physical intimacy—I no longer felt guilt about having sex—but I was still struggling with emotional intimacy. On some level, I was trying to be the perfect priest within a relationship. In other words, I wanted my partner to be vulnerable and confess her failures and faults to me. But I struggled with being vulnerable; I didn't want to be the one confessing. I feared rejection. I was afraid that I wouldn't receive absolution from the women I loved.

This is why the coffee shop confession felt so natural to me; I was playing the role of a priest. I hid behind my collar, both figuratively and literally. I was a coward. This was the harsh and sobering truth that Milena was asking me to face.

As I sat at the edge of the bed, I rubbed Milena's thigh through the covers.

She slowly emerged and said, "Frank, I'm so sorry. What I was saying to you was transference. Do you know that term? It means when you redirect the feelings you have from one person to another. When I was talking to you, I was talking to my stepfather and, to a certain extent, to my biological father."

Milena's biological father had abandoned her, and her stepfather had not made her feel loved or accepted.

"Don't get me wrong," she continued, "you're not completely off the hook. I just didn't want to be unfair to you."

She then slowly took off her clothes and playfully said, "Opportunity is still knocking at your door, Dr. DeVito. Just don't be a fucking idiot."

October 1996 / Cambridge, Massachusetts

As I was driving home, I was thinking about my coffee shop confession. Milena greeted me at the door in her Wonder Woman costume—we were planning to go to a neighbor's Halloween party, and I had bought her an exact replica of the costume that Lynda Carter had worn on the TV show. Milena looked miraculous.

She said to me, "I would love to fuck you in that priest suit, but you're not wearing that to the party."

Then she pulled out a Superman costume and commanded me to change into it. As I looked at the costume, I thought it was even closer to my true identity than my priest clerics. Superman was from another planet, and he struggled to fit into life on Earth. He had to construct an alter ego, Clark Kent, as a way to navigate the human world. His real identity was Superman, but he couldn't be open about who or what he was. In many ways, Clark Kent was a cowardly choice, and I was making this choice daily. I hurt the women in my relationships because I felt more comfortable playing the emotionally distant character of Clark. My partners wanted vulnerability and authenticity—this is the greatness of Superman. They wanted me to be the imperfect superhero who was impervious to bullets but not to love and intimacy.

I stared at the costume, realizing that it was the full embodiment of what made life so hard. Superman lived from the heart. He threw himself into the maelstrom of danger because this was who he was. I lived in a world that celebrated Superman but rewarded Clark Kent.

After I put on the costume, I looked into the mirror and said, "Yes."

When I came out of the bedroom, Milena slapped me on the ass and sensually whispered, "You're a natural in tights."

I took her by her shoulders and pulled her close. I reached into her cleavage and slipped my hand over her breast, feeling the erection of her nipple.

I whispered into her ear, "No woman can fill out this costume like you can."

She laughed and replied, "Is that the line that Superman uses on Wonder Woman?"

When we came home from the Halloween party, I was still thinking about my Colombian friend. Milena knew that I was preoccupied with something, and she was able to coax me into sharing my impromptu confession experience at Dunkin' Donuts. She was an atheist but had a deep respect for my spiritual view of the world.

Milena responded, "You saved someone today, and you should be proud of what you did. Superman, you kicked some serious ass today! And that's what I love about you."

I hugged Milena, deeply appreciative for what she had said, but I replied, "But I'm not a priest. That's what bothers me. He left Dunkin' Donuts thinking that he had experienced a miracle, but I had concocted a fake miracle."

Milena looked at me dumbfounded and said, "I'm not a Catholic, and I don't believe in God, but I do believe in life's synchronicities. You were there at that moment for a reason. And let me clue you in on something that you already know: you are still a priest—with or without the collar."

I stared at Milena, admiring the curves of her body as she stood tall in her Wonder Woman costume. I had a deep desire to make love —not to Wonder Woman but to Milena.

After a spectacular night of lovemaking, I was ready to cue the lights, cue the crescendo of the music score, and roll the final film credits. I was convinced that we would be together forever.

But I was wrong. There was no Hollywood ending. We couldn't overcome the damage within ourselves. Milena struggled with bouts of depression because of her demons, and I defaulted to isolating myself because of mine. As in many relationships, the erosion of our love was imperceptible, subtle, and gradual.

In April of 1997, nearly five years after she had moved into my apartment, we separated. It wasn't an angry separation or devastatingly sad. It felt more like the cold crispness of a fall day when you smell the possibility of snow, knowing that winter is coming.

We've remained friends. Milena moved to California and presently works in the nonprofit sector.

LUMINOUS MYSTERY 2

WANT AD

August 1999 / Cambridge, Massachusetts

As I rocked back and forth into Jennifer, a cascade of her long golden brown hair splashed across the bronze skin of her back and then receded like an ocean tide as she continued to undulate beneath me. Jennifer Lopez's song "Waiting for Tonight" was quietly playing in the background.

My Jennifer was very proud of JLo because of their shared Puerto Rican heritage, and physically, they looked like sisters. She even styled her hair and looks after JLo. I knew Jennifer's playlist and anticipated that "Say My Name" by Beyoncé would play next. While I enjoyed the music of both performers, I found it annoying to listen to them during sex.

I knew that Jennifer was about to climax because she began to rapidly twerk before she stretched her body into a slow and long cat-like yoga stretch. I had learned that a woman's cries, moans, and even yelps were not the guideposts for her orgasm. It was the feel of her body that communicated everything.

We were drenched in sweat because it was a very hot summer evening. When we finished, Jennifer lay across my chest, and I could smell her hair—a perfumed scent of freshly cut flowers.

Jennifer Rivera had just finished her undergraduate degree at Boston University (BU), and I had met her when she did her student teaching at Chelsea High School. She was originally from New Jersey, and we shared in common an ethnic and racial mix of Latinx and Italian. Her father was Puerto Rican and her mother was Italian; my mother was Honduran and my father was Italian.

Unfortunately, I had developed a reputation of getting involved with student teachers. Jennifer seemed to know this because she walked up to me one spring day before school started and simply asked me out like she was ordering a cup of coffee. I was happy to oblige because, to use the language of my students, I wanted to "tap that JLo ass."

I was entering the height of my sexual prowess, and while I enjoyed the rush of having sex with different women, on some level they were becoming sexual objects and playthings. I was able to rationalize that I was getting involved with consenting adults. But, deep down, I felt the rumblings of my conscience because I knew that I was being unfair to these women.

Jennifer and I spent the next couple of months dating, even chaperoning the senior prom together. When she graduated from BU in May of 1999, she moved into my apartment for the summer.

November 1998 / Chelsea, Massachusetts

It was a crisp fall morning, and I entered the school's main office at 7:00 a.m. to meet with Principal Franklin Casillas. While I was waiting in his office, I looked around and noticed the screensaver on his computer that read "NO EXCUSES" in big bold letters. When he came in, he invited me to sit down. We were meeting about my application for a yearlong sabbatical.

"Frank, I read through your application, and I noted that you hadn't explained what you were planning to study and how it would benefit the school when you returned. What exactly are you studying?" asked Principal Casillas.

"My plan was to travel and do some writing. I thought that coming back refreshed and rejuvenated would benefit my students. Because I haven't been my best, I feel that I've cheated them. Emotionally, I'm pretty spent," I responded.

"Ok. It's just that we have very clear terms and conditions for the sabbatical. You can't just travel to Europe like Ernest Hemingway, and then write a novel. You need to outline a clear action plan that follows our sabbatical policy," explained Principal Casillas.

When I heard Principal Casillas' words, I felt they embodied everything that had gone wrong at Chelsea High School and in public education. This was the "age of accountability." Student performance would be measured primarily through state assessments. A single paper and pencil test would drive the direction of schools and districts across the country. In Massachusetts, this test was called the Massachusetts Comprehensive Assessment System (MCAS) test. There was nothing comprehensive about it. How could a single test measure the complexity of everything that a student knew and was able to do? I had fallen in love with project-based learning because it provided daily snapshots of what students were learning and what mattered to them.

While it was considered an enlightened component of the Massachusetts Education Reform Act of 1993, MCAS dismantled creativity and innovation in public education. Testing companies made (and continue to make) millions of dollars subjecting primarily Black and brown children to a barrage of tests that had minimal impact on improving the quality of schools. They then created testing curricula, preparation guides, and textbooks and sold these to districts for millions of additional dollars.

The Massachusetts Department of Education used the tests to hold schools and districts accountable for how they were serving students. While this made sense from a policy perspective, it had a devastating impact at the local level. In response to MCAS, Chelsea High School jettisoned the four-schools-within-a-school model and returned to a traditional comprehensive school model in 1998. The rationale was that everyone had to be on the same page to prepare students for MCAS.

There was no more rowing in the Boston Harbor or participating in a Mock Trial competition, because those experiences didn't prepare students for the state test. The irony is that these projects provided extensive evidence of student learning and mastery. Proficiency on the state test simply demonstrates that a student is able to do well on tests.

When the new Chelsea High School opened its doors in September of 1996, it was designed to support smaller learning communities within the school. A prominent feature of the new high school was two towers that provided separate learning spaces for the four small schools while also creating common spaces like the gym, cafeteria, and library. The regression to a comprehensive high school made life difficult both educationally and physically. Students and faculty now had to trek across large sections of the school to get to class rather than stay in the local space of their small learning community. I was constantly late for my classes because I had two minutes to run from one tower to another.

"Aren't you doing a doctoral program in education at BU?" Principal Casillas asked. Then he suggested, "Why don't you write in your application that you want time to work exclusively on your doctoral studies?" Principal Casillas suggested.

I could have used his idea as an effective lie. "That's a great idea," I replied, "but I've already applied for a leave of absence from BU, too." I wanted to get away from everything.

"Frank, I don't understand your plan. What are you doing? You have a very promising career, and you seem very intent on throwing it all away."

I was experiencing a strange déjà vu as I sat in Principal Casillas' office. He didn't look like Cardinal William Plough, but he sounded like him. He didn't know me and did not seem to be particularly interested in why I was taking the sabbatical. I was simply a cog in the wheel that he had to replace with another teacher. This was a common experience among teachers—our leaders relied upon us but knew very little about who we were and why we were in the teaching profession.

Principal Casillas was small in stature and looked like a cross between Napoleon Bonaparte and the actor Humphrey Bogart. He was Cuban and had grown up in Miami. His parents had fled the country during Fidel Castro's rise to power. When he'd become principal in 1997, it was very apparent that we had deep philosophical differences. I did, however, respect his desire to be a good principal. We weren't friends, but we were friendly with each other.

Unfortunately, he was the front man for the BU Management Team, the body responsible for running the Chelsea Public Schools. After BU was invited by the governor to take over the schools in 1989, a response to Chelsea's earlier mismanagement and corruption, the power of the school committee had been suspended, and the committee now served solely in an advisory role. While I believe that the BU/Chelsea Partnership had yielded many benefits for Chelsea, by the late 1990s the BU Management Team acted more like the Vatican than the Vatican: even though they didn't have a strong connection to the Chelsea community, they didn't see the need for community input when they developed educational policies and practices—they simply issued edicts.

September 1999 / Cambridge, Massachusetts

By the end of the summer, Jennifer and I had broken up. We had planned to travel to Spain together because she had enrolled in a graduate Spanish program in Madrid. My sabbatical request had been approved after I agreed to develop project-based curricula to prepare students for the MCAS exam. Doing this was the equivalent of agreeing to do a paint-by-number curriculum for an art school. It was an absurd proposal, but I was looking for an exit ticket. My idea to follow Jennifer to Spain was also absurd. I was disappointed but thankful that she broke it off just before she left. Over the next two years, we reconnected periodically to have casual sex. I had no complaints—except for her music playlist.

October 1998 / Chelsea, Massachusetts

I was in the teachers' planning room correcting tests. The planning room was a beautiful feature of the new high school. It had a combination of long tables, round tables, and individual work stations. In retrospect, it reminds me of the workspace I regularly saw in the reality TV competition *Project Runway*. It was a space designed for artists who wanted to collaborate.

Unfortunately, the space was now a new wineskin for old wine. We defaulted back into the old way of doing things. As I was engaged in the busyness of correcting history exams, a colleague from the history department came over to me. While her clothes weren't disheveled, her demeanor was.

She asked, "Have you heard about Juan? He committed suicide last night."

I struggled to process what she was saying. I stood up and asked, "What do you mean he committed suicide? He's dead?"

She hugged me and gently said, "I know that the two of you were close. I'm sorry. He was a beautiful kid."

As she hugged me, I looked at the wall of my workstation. I had a cartoon that Juan had drawn depicting the defeat of General Hannibal of Carthage by the Roman General Scipio Africanus at the battle of Zama. It was beautifully detailed. It was brilliant. A tsunami of guilt crashed over me because he had given me that cartoon rather than writing the essay for my history test. I gave him a failing grade for the test but extra credit for the cartoon. I felt that I had failed a young Caravaggio.

Juan Hernández always sat in the front row of my class. He would doodle cartoons, and periodically I would look at them. Juan would flash a beautiful smile whenever I told him that his drawings were fantastic. He was a gifted artist.

His family was from Guatemala. He wore wire rim glasses and parted his dark hair in the middle. Other than that, I knew nothing about him. I later heard from colleagues that the bullying Juan was experiencing because he was gay may have led to his suicide.

I was devastated and enraged by Juan's suicide. We had no mechanism for getting to know students. They were completely anonymous. If Juan had attended Pathways or the Bridge School, he would have been part of an advisory group in which a teacher would have had daily opportunities to get to know him deeply. We would have flagged any issues related to bullying and/or provided counseling to address any struggles related to his sexual identity. We also would have built a project-based learning plan around his gifts as an artist, and he would have completed an internship at a local Boston-based art school, gallery, or graphic design firm.

Juan still might have committed suicide, but I would have liked his chances better if he had received the proper support. Juan had been alone, and he died alone. I was no longer going to be complicit in a public education system that engaged in the daily soul crushing of students and teachers.

Enough was enough. I submitted my application for a sabbatical the following week.

September 1999 / Cambridge, Massachusetts

As I smoked my cigar on my back deck, I was missing seeing my students because I was on sabbatical. On some level, I was also missing Jennifer (mostly missing the sex). Something then happened that was a complete surprise. Walking up the steps of my porch was Angelina Rossellini. She looked at me, a little embarrassed, and asked, "Do you mind if I smoke for a while on your porch?"

Angelina was one of Milena's coworkers at Mount Auburn Hospital in Cambridge. I had had a secret crush on Angelina ever since I had met her at a party to celebrate Milena's birthday. I used to call Angelina "the face" because not only could she "launch a thousand ships" but also the entire air fleet of the US Air Force.

Now she laughed as she sat across from me and said, "Do you know that I smoke on your porch all the time? Milena told me it was fine, and even after she moved out, I kept smoking here." Then she looked at me with curiosity and said, "I didn't know you were home. Why aren't you at school? Are you doing a teacher version of cutting class? Do teachers do that?"

"I'm on sabbatical. That's the next best thing," I replied.

"Wow, sabbatical. I could use that. How long are you off?" she asked.

"I'm off for the entire school year. I'm home free until next September," I said with a great sense of relief.

"Aren't you going to miss it?" asked Angelina.

"I'll miss the students but nothing else," I replied.

"Your dating life is going to suffer. Milena told me that you're a stud among the student teachers." She began to laugh and asked, "Where's the JLo girl?"

I was surprised that Angelina knew anything about Jennifer.

"How do you know about her? We broke up. She moved to Spain," I replied.

"Honey, that's what windows are for," she said, knocking on the porch window. "That girl didn't seem to mind walking around in a thong 24/7, or did you require her to wear that as a uniform?"

I burst out laughing and asked, "How often do you smoke out here?"

She cracked a breathtaking smile and replied, "Almost every day. I come here during my work breaks or after work. It's only a five-minute drive from the hospital. I live in Lexington with my parents. I'll do anything to avoid going home."

I studied Angelina carefully as we talked. I was in complete awe of her presence. She had curly strawberry-blonde hair that she usually tied in a tight bun, but today her hair was beautifully draped over her shoulders. She was tall—about five foot nine—and looked like the twin sister of actress Michelle Pfeiffer. I asked Angelina if she wanted a beer.

She replied, "That would be great. Thanks. By the way, now that you no longer have access to your harem of student teachers, will you be dating someone your age? Or are you one of those guys who only goes around with young nymphos."

"I am looking for an older woman to show me the ropes," I replied.

"I would consider volunteering, but I don't date the exes of friends," Angelina said.

I saw an opening and I ran through it. "Why don't you have dinner with me tonight? You're here anyways. I can grill a couple of steaks."

"Do I have to wear a thong?" Angelina asked playfully.

"No, not tonight. But I can make a Victoria's Secret run sometime tomorrow."

Angelina had these beautiful cat eyes, and she studied me closely as she considered my invitation. She then said, "If you get me another pack of cigarettes, I'll stay."

November 1999 / Boston, Massachusetts

When I checked the balance of my bank account, I had $78.46. I didn't have a paid sabbatical, and while I was dating Angelina, I was not managing my money very effectively. I couldn't go back to Chelsea High School because a teacher had already been hired to fill my slot for the year.

I opened up Sunday's edition of the *Boston Globe* and looked through the want ads. I saw an ad that intrigued me: "Whole-School Change Coach for the Turning Points Program at the Center for Collaborative Education, Boston, MA." I understood each word individually, but I had no idea what this position was about. I did find a rudimentary website for the Center for Collaborative Education, or CCE, and all I knew was that it was a non-profit organization that provided some kind of service to schools.

I typed up my resume for the first time in eight years, and I mailed it to CCE. I received a call the Friday before Thanksgiving asking me to come in for an interview the following Tuesday.

CCE was located in a building on the campus of Northeastern University, bordering Roxbury, a historically Black and under-resourced neighborhood in the heart of Boston. I went to the sixth floor, and a very warm middle-aged woman with short red hair greeted me for the interview. Her name was Patricia Davis, and she was the program director for Turning Points. I walked into her office, and two of her colleagues joined us: Martin O'Malley and Megan Sanders. They introduced themselves as coaches for the Turning Points program.

When we began the interview, Patricia asked me what I knew about the position, and I told her I knew very little. She explained that it involved working with staff to redesign their schools according to the Turning Points model, a research-based model for young adolescent learning that was comparable to the Pathways and Bridge School model. When they heard about my teaching experience, they realized that I had hands-on experience developing and teaching innovative curricula and working with students of color. The only question was whether I had the experience to facilitate meetings with staff to guide them through the "whole-school change" process. When Chelsea was restructuring into four schools within a school, I supported the planning and facilitation of staff meetings. They were very attentive as I described my work doing that. I expected more questions, but then Patricia abruptly stood up and explained that they would notify me if I was chosen for the second round of interviews.

I left CCE intrigued by my initial understanding of the scope of work. I wasn't convinced that I had the experience to do the job, but I was hopeful. On the Wednesday before Thanksgiving, David Andrews, the Executive Director of CCE, called me and offered me the position. I was ecstatic but surprised that I didn't have to do a second interview. He told me to go to the office the following Monday to sign a contract. I still had a very limited understanding of what the position was about.

June 2000 / Cambridge, Massachusetts

After my strange encounter with Angelina on my apartment porch, we had begun a turbulent affair. There was an ice queen quality about her that attracted me. I never knew what she was thinking and feeling. When I asked, she routinely dismissed my questions and told me she was fine.

Her personality had different facets that fascinated me. She could act like one of the guys and play pool while drinking several rounds of beers. Or she could dress like she was going to the Academy Awards. One time when we went to a rock concert, she scraped her car against the car of another concertgoer because she was upset that he had cut her off in the parking lot. There was something erotic about the multiple sides of her personality.

Our first sexual encounters were awkward—she studied me cautiously. After a few sessions, she let loose and our sex felt primal. And I loved it. I really loved it.

After ten months of dating, I decided to take the plunge and ask her to get married. At the time, I was thinking that I was ready to be married. I was thirty-six years old and feeling the pressure to settle down. It felt like I was going to a wedding of a friend or colleague every month, and I thought that settling down with Angelina was the right course of action.

In early June, Angelina and I were invited to the Charles Hotel in Harvard Square to celebrate her friend's birthday party. I had arranged to meet with Angelina a little earlier because my plan was to propose marriage. My mother had given me my paternal grandmother's engagement ring. Because the ring was in rough shape (having survived the Great Depression), we had a jeweler remelt the gold band, add white gold around the setting, and polish and reset the diamond. The ring was very modern and very beautiful.

While we were standing at the bar waiting for her friends, Angelina ordered a martini, and I ordered a vodka tonic. She looked stunning in a black strapless cocktail dress that fit snugly and was cut just below the knees with a revealing side slit.

As we sipped on our drinks, I knelt on the floor and proposed. Angelina's face turned fifty shades of red and she stood there stunned. She placed the ring on her finger, and as she raised her hand to look more closely at the ring, her friends converged on her. They began to scream and yell, "Congratulations!" as they held Angelina's hand high in the air. She smiled at me nervously, and I realized that she still hadn't replied. Because she had placed the ring on her finger, I assumed that the answer was yes, but I wasn't sure.

June 2000 / Burlington, Vermont

The day after I proposed, we drove for a previously-arranged weekend getaway at a bed-and-breakfast in Burlington, Vermont. As we were driving, I was chastising myself for not proposing while we were in Vermont, but Angelina had seemed happy to celebrate her engagement with her friends. She was quiet for most of the trip, and I asked her if she was all right. She explained that she was tired from all the celebrating we did the previous night.

After an amazing dinner of sautéed calamari with garlic, cracked pepper, and olive oil, and hanger steak with sweet potatoes, we returned to the bed-and-breakfast.

After we entered the bedroom, Angelina smiled at me as she took off her jeans and blouse. She was wearing a leopard print thong and bra. It was the first time she had worn something this risqué. Her typical lingerie was frozen in time from the 1950s—she never wore the lingerie that I had given her from Victoria's Secret. But tonight she looked and moved like a leopard as she climbed into the bed.

As I crawled on top of her, she looked at me intensely and clawed my back, breaking skin. I lurched up, wondering what she was doing and then she whispered, "Don't be such a pussy." After a night of lovemaking, we fell asleep around 2:00 a.m. When I woke up the next day, I could see my blood stains on the sheets.

I arranged for breakfast to be delivered to the room. It was Angelina's favorite: egg omelet with feta cheese and spinach, and strawberry pancakes with maple syrup.

As I carried the tray into the bedroom, Angelina said, "Frank, why did you have to ruin everything?"

I was confused and asked, "What did I ruin?"

She looked away and then slowly turned to me and said, "I can't do this. Why the fuck did you propose after only ten months? You don't know shit about me, and I don't know you. You're a good fuck in bed. That's all I know at this point."

I looked at Angelina incredulously and asked, "What have we been doing for the past ten months? I thought we were getting to know each other. What do you call this then?"

"Don't be fucking condescending. I'm not one of your nympho student teachers. We hang out, eat, drink, talk, and fuck. I think marriage involves a lot more."

"Well, what do you want? Where did you think all this was going?" I asked.

"Why do you feel the need to define it? Why can't we just be together? What's the rush to marriage? I don't know if I want to be married. You know I have trust issues. And I thought we agreed to take baby steps. Christ, you know I was gang-raped."

Angelina had been gang-raped as a teen in the Chinatown section of Boston. It had become apparent early in our relationship that this episode had caused her to have trust issues with men.

"I'm working through my own shit," she continued, "and then you chuck the mother lode of all shit at me. I'm fucking pissed with you."

I suddenly began to understand why Angelina felt thunderstruck. We had never discussed marriage or our dreams for our lives. I had never told Angelina that I loved her, and she had never shared her feelings for me. Politically, we were polar opposites. She was a staunch Republican and was euphoric when George W. Bush defeated Al Gore in the 2000 election. She had never asked about my work—especially my new job. And I had never asked her about her work. I hated her parents—they were bigots.

And my mom didn't like Angelina. She would say, "I have a bad feeling about that girl." My mom had not been happy when I shared my marriage plans.

As Angelina ate her omelet and pancakes, I realized that she was right. We didn't know each other. We didn't talk about anything that meant anything. We primarily talked about her family and how much she disliked them—that's all I remembered. Angelina was a beautiful stranger who looked like Michelle Pheiffer.

In retrospect, I wondered if my marriage proposal had been an unconscious attempt to sabotage my relationship with her. Her brokenness was calling the priest in me because at some level, I wanted to heal her. I wanted to save her, and she knew this. It enraged her. This was a powerful undertow in our relationship.

Another undertow was that her overwhelming beauty stroked my ego daily. She was a trophy girlfriend, and I wanted to make her my trophy wife. I bathed in the lavish attention she received from men and women, and I reveled in her glory. My stock as an eligible bachelor exploded in the social stock exchange.

The final undertow in our relationship was my desire to be married and to have children. I was thirty-six years old and was eligible to be elected president. I wanted Angelina to be my first lady. She would be Jackie Onassis, and we would raise our own John F. Kennedy Jr. We would be the perfect royal family. We would be an American royal family.

Deep down, I knew that my soul could no longer live this charade. I had a love/hate relationship with the American dream. It was everything I wanted and everything I despised. My soul knew that the marriage proposal was a grenade, and I was the willing suicide bomber.

After breakfast, Angelina broke up with me. We drove home for the next three hours in virtual silence.

I was devastated when I returned to my apartment. Angelina was a complete stranger, but I was still in love with her. And I missed her.

After two weeks of wallowing in self-pity, I received a phone call. Jennifer was on the other line and said, "Hey Frank, I'm in Boston this week. What are you up to right now? Can I come over?"

NEW YORK MINUTE

August 2000 / Manchester, New Hampshire

I was sitting in my room at Saint Anselm Abbey, a Benedictine monastery located on the campus of Saint Anselm College in Goffstown, bordering Manchester, New Hampshire. I was reading a passage by the thirteenth century German mystic Meister Eckhart:

> Spirituality is not to be learned by flight from the world, or by running away from things, or by turning solitary and going apart from the world. Rather, we must learn an inner solitude wherever or with whomsoever we may be. We must learn to penetrate things and find God there.

I sat with the quote. I struggled to find "inner solitude" and to penetrate the meaning of my own life. I was feeling lost because of my failed engagement attempt with Angelina. I wondered whether I was meant to be married. I was also struggling with my own spiritual growth—where was God in this strange thing called life? I had left the seminary to experience a new and expanded priesthood, but was I actually living it? These questions haunted me.

Jack Donovan, my best friend from the North American College in Rome, had called me to ask whether I wanted to join him on a weeklong summer retreat. He had booked a room at Saint Anselm Abbey. Jack was serving as a chaplain and faculty member at Seton Hall

Preparatory School in West Orange, New Jersey. He called me while I was having another sexual interlude with Jennifer. She and I were friends with benefits—getting together for sex every few months. I was growing weary of it. Jack's invitation felt like an offer of water in the desert.

October, 2003 / Queens, New York

I walked down the hallway of the J.H.S. 217 Robert A. Van Wyck, a middle school located in Queens, New York. The hallway and the school were massive. CCE was contracted to implement the Turning Points model at Van Wyck in 2003. The work was funded through the Comprehensive School Reform (CSR) Capacity Building grants. These were federal grants to support states in the improvement of "failing schools," primarily defined as such through state assessments. Van Wyck had been identified as a "failing school" by the New York City Department of Education, or NYCDOE.

I was on my way to meet with a group of teachers to conduct a needs assessment: gathering qualitative data about teachers' perceptions of the strengths and challenges within the school. As I heard my steps echoing loudly through the vast hallway, a man approached me. He was a Black man in his sixties with a rangy build.

He bellowed in a deep voice, "Are you the consultant from Boston?"

"Yes, my name is Frank DeVito," I replied as I reached out to shake his hand.

He gave me a firm handshake and said, "I'm Ernest Jones. I teach sixth-grade social studies. Excuse me for what I'm about to say. I want to be clear—and please don't take this personally—but I find your presence in this building to be offensive. We are not a failing school. It's ridiculous that we're relying on an arbitrary state test to tell us that we're failing."

As I listened to Ernest, I could hear the pain beneath his words, and I had felt this pain as a teacher. The stigma of being a "failing school" had devastating psychological effects on schools and districts across the country.

I replied, "I agree with you. I don't think there's such a thing as a failing school. But I do believe that every school can get better. I'm not offering you a silver bullet for success. I just want to work with you to see how we can get better."

Ernest looked at me quizzically and angrily said, "How can a guy from Boston, who knows nothing—and I mean nothing—about our kids and our staff, be able to help us?"

He did have a point, but I had been presented with this question a hundred times over the past four years.

I replied, "You're right, I don't know anything about your school. That's why I'm meeting with you and your team. I've always found that it helps to get the perspective of an outsider. I don't have the answers. I'm just here to help facilitate the conversations. You're the ones with the answers."

He smiled and said with amusement, "Are you using some Jedi mind trick? Is this the way that you typically talk to staff? You remind me of Deepak Chopra. Are you Indian?"

I explained to him that I wasn't Indian. I had been mistaken as Indian many times over the course of my lifetime. I especially enjoyed when even Indians would speak to me in Hindi.

Ernest continued, "I just want to give you a heads-up that people are not happy. They will talk to you. They may even jump through a few hoops. But they won't get on board with what you're selling."

August 2000 / Manchester, New Hampshire

Jack and I were technically on a silent retreat. We were not allowed to talk during the day, but there were designated hours when we could briefly talk. Of course, Jack and I found ways around this rule.

The monastic schedule was the following:

6:00 a.m.   Lauds, or morning prayer, with chanting
6:30 a.m.   Breakfast

175

8:00 a.m.	Mass with more chanting
8:45 a.m.	Meditation: a reading followed by silence
11:30 a.m.	Lunch
12:30 p.m.	Sext (sixth hour), or noon prayer, with chanting
2:00 p.m.	Rosary
6:00 p.m.	Vespers, or evening prayer, with chanting
6:30 p.m.	Dinner
9:00 p.m.	Compline, or night prayer, with chanting

The monks who lived in the monastery belonged to the Order of Benedict or the Benedictines. The order was built around a way of living developed by Saint Benedict of Nursia in the sixth century. He created a book called the *Rule of Benedict* which was meant to establish a "middle way" between individual freedom and institutional living. Benedict understood that spirituality was primarily relational, and the focus was the building of community among believers. He is considered the father of monasticism in the West. There is a debate about whether Benedict would have sanctioned the establishment of a religious order; his book was meant to guide individuals and existing informal communities.

I prayed to Saint Benedict to help me to find the "middle way" in my own life. I still hadn't found that sweet spot of being fully divine and fully human. I went from being a virgin for most of my young adult life to being Giacomo Casanova, resolved to make up for lost time. "Ora et labora" (pray and work) is the Benedictine motto. Benedict knew that everything we do is a form of prayer. His rule book was a practical structure to remind us of this.

I used the retreat time to reflect upon the rules that were operative in my own life.

Humor was an important rule in my life. During dinner, I was trying to make Jack laugh by taking my napkin and making it into a puppet. When I took a walk with Jack across the campus of the monastery and Saint Anselm College, Jack and I recounted our funny seminary stories.

But I told him nothing about Sophie, Francesca, Jessica, Hilary, Milena, Jennifer, or Angelina. He knew of them, but knew nothing about them. He was my best friend, and I told him nothing— absolutely nothing. He knew nothing about my deepest joys and my most devastating pain. *Invulnerability* was an operative rule in my life.

I thought about the healing of Diego at Our Lady of Lourdes, buying Celina her prom dress, and listening to the Columbian man's confession in the coffee shop. *Compassion* was one of my rules.

I craved silence and reflection. I needed time away from people. I wanted just to sit still. *Praying* was one of my rules.

I had written a bogus sabbatical plan, and I didn't tell my students the real reasons why I was leaving. And I soft-pedaled hard conversations with the women I loved. *Avoiding conflict* was an operative rule in my life.

As I continued to reflect on the rules operating in my life, I realized that while I was a flawed person, I was still walking the path of a human and divine life. I had focused upon my own shortcomings and allowed these to overshadow the ways I had grown and expanded. I was still on the path, and I was committed to keep walking.

October, 2003 / Queens, New York

Ernest led me to a classroom where I would meet one of the sixth-grade teams. The teachers had arranged the desks in a circle, and we introduced ourselves. Ernest was on the team, and he taught social studies. Paula was a young white teacher who taught English. Matt was also a young white teacher, and he taught math. Carmen was a middle-aged Latinx woman who taught science. After we did our introductions, I gave them some background about why I was there and what I was hoping to accomplish during the meeting. I also checked in with them to see if they understood why I was there. We then began our discussion.

"We don't have a lot of time together, and I just want to propose three ground rules for our discussion." I took a piece of chart paper that was folded in my backpack and placed it in the middle of the floor.

It read:

(1) Listen to understand—don't rush to judgement: focus on what others are saying;

(2) Speak your truth—speak what you honestly think and feel in your heart; and

(3) Ask questions—don't make assumptions about what others are thinking or feeling.

I then turned to the group and asked them if they would like to add any other ground rules.

Carmen replied, "Have fun. I think that's a good ground rule. We can take the work seriously but not take ourselves so seriously."

I loved Carmen's suggestion. I bent down to the floor and added it to our ground rules. The team gave the ground rules a thumbs up.

"If our goal is improvement, we need to be clear about what we're reaching for—what we want our students, staff, and families to experience each day. We need to be clear about what a great school looks, sounds, and feels like," I explained. "Before we have that discussion, I would like to talk about what students, staff, and families are currently experiencing. If it's ok with you, let's start with families," I suggested. "If your child were going to this school, and you walked into the school—what would you see? Try to be as concrete as possible."

"I would see love," replied Ernest.

I asked Ernest what love looked like to him.

He continued, "I would see teachers greeting students as they came in, and they would say things like, 'How's your day, young man?' And as the students left your classroom, I would hear, 'Have a wonderful day.'"

Matt, the math teacher, replied, "On the walls, I would see the work that my child was doing in the classroom." I asked him why that was important to him. He replied, "I want to know that my kid is not wasting his time. I'm not a parent, but I would hope to see that my kid was working on something worthwhile."

"I would see kids having fun," Paula, the English teacher, piped in. I asked her what fun looked like to her. "You know, kids laughing with big smiles on their faces."

I asked Carmen, the science teacher, what she would see as a parent. She looked down and then said, "I'm not sure whether my team is ready to hear my truth." She reached into her pocketbook and popped a piece of peppermint candy in her mouth. Her colleagues encouraged her to talk.

"Let's get real about this. No teacher here would send their child to this school, and that's the problem," Carmen said with conviction. Ernest protested and announced to the group that he would have sent his kids. He explained that he had five kids and they had all attended New York City public schools.

"Yeah, but where do you live, Mr. Jones? Me and Mr. Jones go way back, and he knows that your zip code determines the quality of your school. Our teachers don't live in the zip codes where our students are from, and that's the honest-to-goodness truth."

Ernest was groaning in disagreement as Carmen spoke. I reminded the group about our ground rules. I asked Carmen to share what she would see.

"I would see well-intentioned teachers who would try to mold my child into something he's not."

I asked Carmen to give an example.

She continued, "OK, we give assignments every day, and we expect our kids to complete them. If they do it, they get an A, and if they don't, we give them an F. We do this day in and day out. I know in my heart that if I was a parent, the teachers in this school would not know my child. I'm not saying that they're bad people. I'm just saying that they have good intentions and that's about it."

August 2000 / Manchester, New Hampshire

After dinner, Jack was able to track down cigars and some bottles of beer. We sat on a couple of chairs in a field outside the monastery and enjoyed a smoke and a drink.

Being with Jack reminded me of the TV comedy *Seinfeld*, famously known as the "show about nothing." Jack and I had crafted a very entertaining friendship about nothing. I loved it, but I wanted more.

While we were puffing on cigars and sipping our beer, I asked, "Do you realize that we talk about nothing? We've been friends for over thirteen years, and we've never really talked. Have you ever noticed that?"

Jack looked at me like I had just stepped out of an alien spacecraft and said, "Are you fucking yanking my chain?"

He continued, "Is this a serious question? I have no idea what you're talking about. Right now you sound like Antonio De Luca."

Antonio De Luca was a theology professor at the Gregorian University, in Rome.

"Remember that prick?" he asked. "Remember the bullshit he used to spew on us: 'God is found in nothingness. And nothingness is found in God.' And, of course, you volunteered me to be the notetaker for that bullshit course."

I remembered Antonio De Luca, and I liked his class. I went off course a bit to defend him.

"De Luca's class was great. It was thought-provoking. His description of God resonated with my experience. Did you notice that he was the only professor who ever asked us what it felt like to experience God?"

Jack started laughing and motioned his hands to form quotation marks: "'Thought-provoking.' That's your classic MO, Frank. You've always loved that shit. Remember in Rome when you dragged me to the Pasquino to see *Breakfast with Shakespeare*? That Euro-shit movie where two guys were rolling around in Captain Crunch."

This was the Jack that I loved, but I knew we could be more.

"Jack, why did you decide to be a priest?"

He rolled his eyes and replied, "You know my story. I've told it to you a hundred times."

"I don't remember it. If you told it to me a hundred times, wouldn't I have remembered something?

Jack replied, "OK, I'm going to oblige your bullshit just this once. My mother died from cancer when I was in high school. I don't know how the fuck you could forget that," he exclaimed indignantly. "She had a devotion to the rosary when we were growing up. It rubbed off on me. When she died, I found a lot of comfort in our Blessed Mother. She was there for me when I needed Her."

"So Mary was like your surrogate mother?" I asked.

"Yes, Dr. Fucking Freud. Mary had a special place in my life, and I wanted to dedicate my life to Her. That's when I felt the calling to the priesthood."

We sat there in silence. After Jack spoke, I realized that the priesthood was the first woman in my life. She was my first lover. It wasn't the Church or Jesus or Mary. It was the priesthood.

Jack then asked me, "Can I ask you a question, Dr. Freud? Why did you leave the seminary? I know it had something to do with your dick, but you never told me the full story."

"Well, you know about my story with Sophie. That was one reason. The other reason is harder to describe. Before I get into it, I want you to know something: when I walk into a church and smell the candle wax and the remnant scent of incense, I feel like a ballplayer walking onto a baseball field where I can smell the grass and the popcorn from the stands. Like a ballplayer loves baseball, I love the priesthood."

Jack sat up in his chair and said, "So why the fuck did you leave? I don't get it."

"Like I said, it's hard to explain. I was feeling a calling. It felt like love: it was a love beyond the Vatican. I felt born again, and I couldn't go back into the womb of the world I knew."

As I spoke to Jack, I was struggling to find words for a calling that I didn't fully understand. I was not trying to reimagine the ordained priesthood as defined by the Catholic Church. I did not leave because I was upset with the hierarchy or the dysfunction of the institution. These were things that I had known about the Church my entire life.

I felt that my soul was expanding, and the ordained priesthood was no longer aligned to this expansion. I still felt called to a priesthood, but the focus was no longer on being a leader within a church community, but a leader within a local community. My understanding of what constituted this local community was still undefined. My experience as a teacher in Chelsea felt like a priesthood—this was an example of a new community I served. But my soul was expanding beyond Chelsea.

In the end, all I knew was that the new community needed to align with the expansion of my soul.

"You are now officially scaring me. You are starting to sound like fucking Antonio De Luca. You're talking in circles. What are you talking about?" Jack asked with reverent sarcasm.

"I'm not trying to be an asshole about this. I'm trying to find the words to describe it. OK, here we go: do you know why a snake sheds its skin?"

"What am I—National Geographic? I have no fucking idea. Can you stop channeling De Luca and get to your point?" Jack insisted.

"A snake sheds its skin not only to make room for new skin but also to destroy the parasites that have lodged themselves into the old skin. My understanding of the priesthood was expanding. I was shedding skin, and I was concerned about the parasites I saw in the Church's understanding of the priesthood—the privilege and the sense of entitlement. I don't believe this was the dream of Jesus," I explained.

From my perspective, privilege and entitlement were not the sole domain of the Catholic Church. They were powerfully present in any institution and community. Shedding skin was not a one-time event— it was a painful process that I surrendered to regularly over the course of my life.

"I see. So now you are officially the pope. You get to decide what Jesus intended. That's very convenient. You've always wanted to do things your way, and now you can do it," Jack said in frustration.

"Fuck you, Jack. Anything you can't wrap your head around you shit on. Yeah, I am channeling Antonio De Luca, and if you had just listened to him for one goddamn minute, you would get it. Remember the last supper, Jack? Jesus washes the feet of the disciples, and he tells them to do the same. At that moment, Jesus is shedding some serious skin. Love does not reside in institutions or authorities. Love resides in service. The Church doesn't own love. It doesn't own life. No fucking institution owns love or life."

Jack was quiet. We sat in silence smoking and drinking. For the first time, we were adhering to the monastic silence rule.

Jack finally broke the silence, "So is it all bullshit? The Church? The priesthood? Was it all a fucking a waste of time?"

"I didn't say that. The Church is a community. I believe that religion and spirituality are relational. The Church is a structure to support community. I'm not saying that your life is a fucking waste if that's what you're worried about. Jack, the last supper was the ultimate expression of community. As a priest, you're facilitating that experience for others. I'm just saying that love, community, and life extends beyond any church or institution. I believe that was Jesus' point."

"Yeah—a fucking love beyond the Vatican." Jack chimed as he smiled.

August 2000 / Manchester, New Hampshire

Ernest was upset that Carmen had broken ranks with the team. There was a tension in the room, but it was primarily between Ernest and Carmen. It was a veteran teacher standoff, and Carmen was winning. Both Ernest and Carmen had grown up attending New York City public schools. They had worked together at Van Wyck for over fifteen years. I reminded the team about our ground rules and continued the conversation.

"I want you to remember yourself as an adolescent, as a middle school student. If you were a student at this school, what would you hope to experience? What would it look, sound, or feel like? Try to be as detailed as possible."

Paula replied, "I loved to dance. My parents tried to get me into one of the performing arts schools, but I wasn't accepted. They paid for dance lessons after school, but I was thinking that dance would be a great activity in this school. Gym should be more than gym. Why can't it be dance?"

"I would have wanted my teachers to see me in a different way," replied Ernest.

I asked Ernest to explain what he meant.

"Because I was tall," he said, "I was always told that I should try out for basketball. They never asked me what I wanted to do. I wanted to be an archaeologist. I guess my dream was fulfilled—I'm a dinosaur now in this school."

The group broke into a round of laughter.

Carmen replied, "I always loved science as a kid. I had an experience like Ernest: none of my teachers encouraged me to pursue science. They didn't think I had the aptitude. I had a high school teacher who did encourage me to become a teacher. I'm living the dream—I'm a scientist and a teacher. For this school, I wish my students had more projects. My kids love projects."

"Do I have permission to swear?" Matt looked to the team for their consent and they amusedly gave it. "As a kid, I just liked fucking around. Experimenting with shit. There's no opportunity to get messy in this school. I mean, they're kids. We expect them to be sitting down for six hours? I could never sit down for that long."

As the meeting ended, the team thanked me, and we scheduled a meeting for the following month. I told them that I was going to type up my notes, and I assured them that they would be part of a larger conversation about the direction that they wanted for the school.

Ernest, my resident doubting Thomas, warned me, "Look, Frank, I can see what you're trying to do, but our school is Grand Central Station for consultants. What you're doing will get lost in the mix."

Carmen came up to me and said, "That's the first meaningful conversation that I've had in a long time. Thank you, Mr. Frank. Have a safe trip home, and I'll see you next month."

As I was packing up, Paula asked me, "Frank, can I ask you a personal question? Why did you leave the classroom?"

I had been asked this question many times, but in this moment, it felt like the first time.

"I came to a point when I knew it was time to move on," I told her. "I had taken a sabbatical and run out of money, and I basically stumbled onto this job. I started enjoying this work, and I told my principal that I wasn't going back. He wasn't disappointed."

"Do you think you'll ever go back?" Paula asked.

"I don't know. I find that life usually kicks me through a door, and then when I turn around, the door is locked. I don't know what's behind the next door," I replied.

As Patricia was leaving she asked, "How long will you be in New York? If you stay long enough, you'll find out that Don Henley and the Eagles were right, 'Everything can change in a New York Minute.'"

I wasn't quite sure what to make of Patricia's comment. But something about it rang true.

CARNAVAL IN THE SUBWAY

February, 2003 / Rio de Janeiro, Brazil

I stared out into the darkness and saw my reflection in the window as our subway train was accelerating. I shifted my attention to a group of teenagers who were dressed in elaborate Maya costumes. Large fans of peacock plumes were twisting and turning on their heads as they engaged in animated conversations. It was the first night of Carnaval in Rio de Janeiro, Brazil, in 2003. The crowds were starting to head home around 4:00 a.m., but it didn't feel late. The energy was still pulsating through the train cars. I was with my friends Adriana Oliveira and Sergio Sousa—they were my guides for the trip.

Adriana was sitting next to me, and I said to her, "It's funny. I've only seen Maya dress in textbook pictures and history documentaries. I've never seen it in person. On my mother's side, we have Maya ancestry. I thought that I was the last of the Maya," I jokingly protested.

One of the teenagers overheard me and asked me, "Sir, are you Maya?"

"Yes, on the Honduran side of my family," I replied.

"What do you think of our costumes? Are they accurate?" he asked.

"I can sleep well tonight because you did a great job representing my people. I thank you, and my ancestors thank you."

Adriana and Sergio shook their heads in amused disbelief as they listened to the conversation.

"So you guys performed tonight?" I asked.

A few more teenagers joined our conversation and they replied, "Yes, we performed in Leblon [a neighborhood near Copacabana]. Would you like to see us perform?"

Before I could say yes, the train car rumbled with loud percussion, screeches and whistling, and singing and dancing as the teens began to samba. They were banging on the ceiling of the train car and inviting passengers to stand up and dance with them. Growing up, I had always enjoyed musicals because I loved to imagine a world where random strangers would spontaneously break into singing and dancing. I was now living a Brazilian musical.

As I was soaking in the spectacle, I turned to Adriana and said, "This is fantastic."

She smiled and replied, "In Brazil, happiness is a choice."

June 2002 / Cambridge, Massachusetts

"Why can't we get the frame right for this shot? I want to see the beds!" barked Carlos Silva, a film director. Carlos was from Recife, Brazil, and he had just completed a film and media arts degree at Emerson College in Boston. He was directing a film called *A Fronteira* (The Border) that dramatized the immigration stories of two Brazilian families making the dangerous journey across the Mexican border into the United States. I was asked by my friend João Antunes, who was one of the film's producers, to serve as an extra on the film.

I had received a call from João after a disastrous morning meeting with a group of middle school teachers in South Boston. João explained that it was an emergency, and his film crew was in desperate need of extras. I was able to recruit my brother Anthony and my Uncle Mario, who was visiting from Honduras. We were asked to go to a homeless shelter in Cambridge. João had arranged to use the bedroom space for the day, and they were using it as an immigration detention center in the movie. We were given prison-like clothes because we would play immigrants who had been caught at the Texas border. In the scene that was being filmed, the main character had just been caught and arrested by the US Border Patrol. We would be standing or lying on the beds of the detention center while the action was happening.

While we were waiting for the filming to start, Anthony and Uncle Mario were asked to lay down on the stark metal beds. I was assigned to stand at the foot of the beds, smoking a cigarette. As a cigar smoker, this was difficult because I hated the taste of cigarettes. They tasted like rolled up newspaper doused in Lysol.

My uncle Mario then said to me, "Francis, do you know that I am a prisoner in my own life?"

"What do you mean?" I reluctantly asked. I knew that a monologue was coming.

"I like the subtitle of this movie, *Ninguém é ilegal* (Noone is Illegal). I'm made to feel illegal everyday. I live in a country [Honduras] where my rights as a human being are not recognized. We have a president. We have a constitution. We even have something like a bill of rights on paper. But I am not free. And my brothers and sisters are not free. I am not acting in this movie. This is my real life."

Mario was the younger brother of my mother, Candida. He was a Renaissance man: an engineer, a philosopher, a writer, and a communist. Unfortunately, he struggled with depression and alcohol addiction. If his life were made into a play, it would be called *A Honduran Tragedy*.

My uncle was the ultimate symbol of broken dreams and unrealized potential. This scared me because I wondered if I could end up like him. I loved my uncle and regardless of his struggles, I still admired him. Every time I looked at him, I was reminded of who he was, and who he could have been.

As I gazed at my uncle with deep love and compassion, Carlos asked me to light a cigarette because the scene was starting.

June 2002 / South Boston, Massachusetts

Earlier in the day, before I was invited to be in the film shoot, I'd had an 8:00 a.m. meeting with a group of white male middle school teachers in their sixties. We met in the teachers' room, and before the meeting, they went to the coffeemaker and poured cups of coffee into styrofoam cups and loaded their coffees with powdered dairy creamer and sugar.

They were the members of the eighth-grade academic team. I had been working with the team on developing a literacy approach in their classrooms to guide students to access the different types of texts that they were required to read: fiction and non-fiction narratives, math word problems, and history and science texts.

I dreaded this meeting because I had worked with this group for a year and had nothing to show for it. We were going to use a meeting protocol called "Looking at Student Work." A teacher would present a work sample from a student and present a problem and/or question. We would then examine the work and ask a series of questions to help a teacher to reflect on their practice and develop next steps.

Arnie Benton, a math teacher, handed out copies of a math assignment and student work samples to the group. I asked Arnie to present his question to the team.

"My question is: how can I stop being a remedial math teacher? I mean, these kids are so far behind—they can barely add and subtract," Arnie said.

"Arnie, your question is pretty big. Remember that this protocol works well when we can focus on something more specific. What's the particular problem with the math assignment and the student work you just circulated?" I asked.

"There's nothing wrong with my math assignment. It's the kids that are the problem. I mean, they cannot focus for even one minute to do a simple assignment."

As I was listening to Arnie, I was getting angry. This was the type of toxic conversation that we had been having all year, and I felt complicit in allowing them to continue.

"Arnie, remember our ground rule about focusing on what we can control? What can you control in regard to this assignment?" I asked.

"I can't control anything! That's my point. In my humble opinion, what we're doing here is a massive waste of our time. When these kids leave this school, the best they'll be able to do is flip burgers."

I lost it. I completely lost it.

"Arnie, you're the one who should be flipping burgers. I should be calling the police because what you do day-to-day is so criminal. You're always talking about what your kids can't do, and not once have I ever heard you talk about what they can do. And I consider that intellectual and moral laziness. You're absolutely right. I have fucking wasted my time and your time. If I were a parent of one of these kids, I would smash your head through the fucking wall."

The room was silent. All I could hear was the quiet slurping of coffee.

June 2002 / Cambridge, Massachusetts

After seventeen takes, Carlos was finally satisfied with the detention center scene. We broke for lunch, and my friend João invited us to have some sandwiches. One of the actresses, Adriana Oliveira, smiled at me and served me a sandwich. She grew up in São Paulo, Brazil, and was very attractive—long straight dark hair, large brown eyes, and an electric smile. I could feel the Hulk begin to growl within me, but I decided to remain Bruce Banner. We began talking, and she explained that she was a theatre actor and had done some TV commercials. This was her first major film role.

As we were talking, the actor who played the main character of the film, Sergio Sousa, joined our conversation. He was originally from Rio de Janeiro and was primarily a character actor in some popular Brazilian soap operas. He was good-looking—not in the pretty boy sense—but he had a presence.

I was fascinated with the craft of acting, and we began a conversation.

"What's your approach to acting? Method acting? Are there other approaches?" I asked.

Sergio replied, "I don't use what you call Method acting. That approach is a little too self-conscious for me."

Adriana nodded her head in agreement.

I said, "As you know, Marlon Brando is considered the greatest American actor, and he was supposedly a Method actor. I'm curious. Are you saying that his performances were too self-conscious?" I asked.

"I don't mean to pooh-pooh Marlon Brando, but I don't consider him a great actor for the reason you just gave. He was too self-conscious. What I mean is that in his films you can see him grasping for the identity of his character. He never looked natural to me, and I found this distracting.

"For me, acting is about authenticity," he explained. "It's about looking natural. It's not about grasping for a character. Even in his famous movie when he said, 'I could have been a contender,' he was actually looking out of the car and reading a cue card. Did you know that? He was horrible at remembering his lines."

"Wow, you're dissing Brando? So who are some great actors in your mind?" I asked.

"I love Jimmy Stewart. He's one of my favorites. His characters look so natural. I'm able to get lost in the reality of his movies because I believe in his authenticity. My favorites tend to come from the Golden Age of Hollywood: Gary Cooper, Kirk Douglas, and Clark Gable. Do you know who was a very underrated actor? Cary Grant. He could do dramas and comedies and make it look so natural, so easy. Do you know how hard it is to make something look easy? Because it looks easy, we assume it was easy. It takes work."

"So what is your process? How do you make your acting look natural?" I asked.

"First of all, the key is to remind myself that I am not acting. Before we began filming today, I heard what your uncle said to you. He said something to the effect that he felt like a prisoner in his own life, and that the movie represented his real life. By the way, I'm sorry to hear that. But what your uncle said is our process. We look at the reality of the story—even if it's science fiction. Regardless of the story, there is always something very real. As human beings we are all connected to the real: to love, hatred, fear, and anger. I don't have to act, because I have felt the emotions of my character. All I have to do is be myself in order to be that character. In the end, we are all one."

Adriana, Sergio, and I enjoyed our conversation so much that we became friends, and we spent a lot of time together over the summer. They had agreed to remain in Boston to promote the film. Just before they left for Brazil in the fall of 2002, they invited me to join them in Rio for Carnaval that coming February.

June 2002 / South Boston, Massachusetts

My meeting ended abruptly with the eighth-grade team. I excused myself and walked towards the principal's office to explain what had happened. As I was walking down the hallway, a security officer intercepted me and notified me that I was to leave the school's premises immediately. He escorted me to the front door.

Principal Michael Cohen was waiting just outside the entrance. He said to me, "Frank, I will be contacting CCE to request that you be removed as our coach. What you did was egregious and unacceptable. I don't think an apology will work. I'm sorry it happened. Good luck with everything." He then quickly entered the building.

As I was getting into my car, my cell phone began to vibrate. It was my friend João. He told me about the emergency casting call for extras for his film.

While driving to Cambridge to join the film crew, I thought about what had transpired. Principal Michael Cohen and the eighth-grade team were old Boston. This was the old boys' club in the Boston Public Schools. As the school system was becoming more progressive in its policies and practices, the old boys' club was seeing the slow decline of their fiefdoms. They could no longer hide like mobsters in the shadows—the light was chasing them.

I almost lost my job over the incident. While CCE was sympathetic to my case, I was formally reprimanded for not handling it well.

As my rage for that South Boston teacher subsided, I felt sorry for him. I realized that I was just mirroring the way he was treating his students—I dismissed him. He was just another racist good ol' boy, riding in a pickup truck. He was more than this, but I lacked the intellectual and moral resolve to know him better. I preferred to leave him as a character actor in my personal theatre.

February, 2003 / Rio de Janeiro, Brazil

As we were exiting the train station, I noticed that the teens dressed as Maya were heading towards the *favelas*. These were large neighborhoods of slums that bordered nicer sections of Rio de Janeiro. Homes and buildings were poorly and dangerously constructed. Both organized and disorganized crime was rampant. As I was staring at the teens walking to the favelas, Adriana said to me, "I told you. In Brazil, happiness is a choice."

April 2003 / Somerville, Massachusetts

I was excited about the premiere of the film *A Fronteira*. The film would be screened in movie cinemas in Somerville and then Revere. I had never been to a movie premiere party, and I was excited by the pulsating energy as I entered the cinema. I was walking with Adriana and Sergio, and most folks thought that I was an actor in the film. I didn't correct them. I was happy to sign autographs and take photos with fans. I was in the film—I just didn't have any speaking lines.

My joy quickly waned when the movie started.

The movie was a noble failure. It was ok but not great. There were sections when the film stuttered, and the editing was not sharp but choppy.

Sergio was brilliant in his scenes. He appeared natural, and I did forget that he was acting. Adriana was also very good. I cringed at a very graphic scene in which she was raped at the border by a *coyote* (a person paid by immigrants to smuggle them across the Mexican border into the United States). I wasn't expecting it, and I found it deeply disturbing. I wondered how Adriana prepared for this scene. She never discussed it.

I laughed when I saw my scene—I wasn't smoking. After seventeen takes, Carlos knew that I didn't look natural with a cigarette.

Unfortunately, the audience laughed during scenes that were meant to be serious. During one scene, a drug dealer went into a pizzeria and threatened to call immigration on Sergio's character, who was working behind the counter. He was a white actor dressed as a rapper, and he was so over-the-top in the scene that the cinema erupted with laughter. I also busted a gut laughing when Sergio leaned over and told me that the actor who played the drug dealer taught acting classes at Emerson College. I would have demanded a refund.

As I was watching the movie, I was thinking of the teens in Rio who had dressed up as Maya for Carnaval. Their performance on the train completely trumped what I was watching on the screen. I was wondering whether they were still choosing happiness in the favelas.

FRAGILE TRINITY

March 2003 / São Paulo, Brazil

As I was waiting at the ticket counter at São Paulo/Guarulhos International Airport, I wasn't ready to leave Brazil to go home. The rhythms of the country were still vibrating in my body, and my mind was haunted by the vision of the Maya-dressed teens celebrating on the car of the subway train.

As I handed my ticket and passport to a very attractive airline agent, she cracked a warm smile and asked, "So you're an American? And you're going back to Boston?"

I said yes to both questions.

"Did you enjoy your stay?" she asked. I stood there for a few seconds and didn't say anything. Because the line was long, I could hear the groans of the people waiting behind me.

"Are you ok, sir? Can I help you?" she asked in a concerned and kind way.

I tapped on the counter and asked incoherently, "If I were to stay, I mean if I accidentally lost my tickets—duh, the tickets are here—but I mean if you pretended not to see them…and I just left the line?"

She leaned into me, and I could smell her floral perfume as she said with a flirty smile, "Sir, I'm happy to accomodate you. I'm a full-service customer representative. I could delay the date of your return trip." She continued, "Would you need assistance in finding a place to stay? My shift ends in a few hours. I could help you at that time."

I could see she was getting the wrong idea, and I had no complaints.

As the Hulk rumbled within me, Dr. Bruce Banner asserted himself, "Forget it. I'll check my baggage."

April 2003 / Boston, Massachusetts

I was still feeling disoriented after my trip to Brazil. I needed to talk to someone. I called my friend Camila Ramirez. I had been introduced to Camila through a close friend when they came to my birthday party in August of 2001.

From the time I met Camila, I had been deeply attracted to her. She was originally from Puerto Rico, and she had ivory skin, penetrating brown eyes, and a luxurious mane of wavy red hair that extended to the middle of her back. My attraction was not only physical. She was studying to be a clinical psychologist, and she was working on her doctorate. We connected on an emotional and spiritual level that gave me hope that love was still possible for me.

I was disappointed to learn that she had a partner—Gabriela Sanchez. They had been together for four years, and Gabriela was also completing her doctorate in clinical psychology. They had met at the University of Puerto Rico. Gabriela was also a strikingly beautiful woman. She had long, straight black hair and smoky blue eyes that were hypnotic. As a couple, they were beautiful in every way.

Camila agreed to meet me for dinner. Camila and Gabriela had an apartment on Boylston Street in Boston. It was a great location between Copley Plaza, the Prudential Center, and the Fenway neighborhood (a.k.a. the home of the Boston Red Sox). We went to a Cuban restaurant a few miles from her home.

As we waited to order, Camila shined a ridiculously glorious smile as she said, "Frank, I can see and feel that there's something very different about you. Brazil has changed you. What happened?"

"I don't know if I could put it into words," I replied. I then shared with Camila my experience of seeing the teens dressed as Maya on the subway train.

I continued, "In that moment, I felt like, for a few brief minutes, I saw the heart of life. It was life itself beating in front of me. When I realized that these kids were from the favelas, I felt ashamed. When I wake up in the morning, I'm always complaining in my mind about something. Nothing is ever really good enough. I'm not good enough at my job. I'm not good enough as a son and brother. I'm not good enough as a friend. I'm not good enough as a lover. I'm not good enough."

I took a sip of the Rioja wine we had ordered and continued, "Then I saw those kids—those fucking kids. They were like little buddhas dancing in front of me. At that moment, I felt like I knew nothing about life."

Camila took my hand and gently said, "Frank, look at me. The reason why you appreciated what those kids were doing was because you are one of them. You are that kid. You are that buddha. Only a kid could have appreciated the miracle you were witnessing."

I wanted to cry but I couldn't—not even in front of Camila. I trusted her, but I couldn't let go.

Then she said, "You've always led with your heart, and that's why we're friends. I connected to your heart. I don't believe that you found your heart in Brazil. I believe that you received validation to live from and through your heart. We all need that validation because we live in a world that mistrusts the heart. We need to develop plans. We need to develop goals and timelines. We'll do anything to avoid matters of the heart."

"Wow, Dr. Ramirez. You are good. You are really good," I said, doing a mock imitation of Robert De Niro's character in the film *Analyze This*. "How much do I owe you?"

After my dinner with Camila, I started spending a lot of time with her and Gabriela. We would spend hours in their apartment drinking wine and talking about subjects close to my heart: psychology, philosophy, and spirituality.

I asked about a subject that had been taboo for me for most of my life, "How do the two of you understand sexuality? You're in a relationship with each other and you're both studying to be clinical psychologists. I'm wondering what you've learned."

They both arched their backs with excitement in anticipation of the conversation.

Gabriela leaned in and began, "Well first of all, sexuality is an incredibly complex subject. Unfortunately, our culture in the west tends to reduce and even conflate the biological and psychological aspects of sex and gender identity. When we tease out the categories of sexual identity and gender, there are six categories, and within each category, there is a wide spectrum. When you think about the possible combinations, you have hundreds—if not thousands—of combinations in relation to sexual identity and gender."

I almost choked on a large sip of wine as Gabriela spoke. She spoke about sexual identity like she was an explorer in an undiscovered country, and for a brief moment, I was embarrassed. However, I was fascinated, and I asked about the categories and combinations.

Camila chimed into the conversation, "First you have biological sex—the Xs and Ys of your chromsomes. Like Gabriela said, there is a wide spectrum between male and female. You can have an extra chromosome—extra Xs or extra Ys—that affect your biological gender. Second, you have gender identity or your psychological understanding of your gender: do you think and feel as a male or female or anything in between? And third," she continued, "gender expression—how you present yourself to the world. I have a professor who comes in as Mark on some days and Margarita on other days. He is biologically male, and his gender identity and expression are both male and female."

Wow, I felt like I should be paying tuition at this point.

Gabriela jumped in again, "The fourth category is sexual identity. This is usually reduced to gay or straight, but there is such a large spectrum. You could be bisexual, pansexual, and/or anything in between. The fifth category is sexual attraction—are you attracted to males, females, and again, everything in between."

She went on, "And the final category is sexual behavior—how you live out your sexual identity and your particular attractions. Because you identify as bisexual may not mean that you're bisexual in practice."

Camila and Gabriela rolled over on the couch, laughing as they looked at my shell-shocked expression.

For several weeks after that, I was steeped in my graduate studies in sexual identity and gender with Camila and Gabriela.

I was also very happy to return to my evenings of dancing salsa and merengue. When I was dating a doctoral student in philosophy in the mid-1990s, she introduced me to the Latin dance scene in Cambridge and Boston. I had given it up the past few years, but Brazil inspired me to return to the floor. As I was heading home from a night of dancing, Camila called me on my cell phone.

"I'm sorry for calling so late. Are you home right now?"

I explained to her that I was heading home and I needed a shower because I was drenched in sweat from a night of dancing.

She then said, "Gabriela and I would love to see you. You're welcome to take a shower here. There's something important that we wanted to talk to you about. Have you eaten? We have some veggies, pita, and hummus."

"Is everything ok?" I looked down at my watch and saw that it was 12:30 a.m. "I can come over. That's not a problem."

I was buzzed into the apartment building and took the stairway to the second floor. Their apartment door was already open when I arrived. I called out for them as I went through the door.

Camila came over and gave me a very warm hug and kiss. Gabriela did the same.

They lived in a loft style apartment with tall ceilings, a wide open floor, and large windows. I could see the city lights shining through the window panes. The decor of their apartment was very sensual—soft red, orange, and yellow colors could be found throughout: in the paintings that hung on the walls, in the curtains, the throw rugs, the table covers, and the candles.

I smelled sandalwood incense as Camila invited me to sit on the couch. Gabriela brought over a platter of pita bread, veggies, and hummus. Camila then asked me to open up a bottle of Rioja wine, and I poured a glass for each of us. Their orange couch was L-shaped, and they sat together on the long end, holding each other's hands, and I sat on the short end.

Camila then said, "Frank, we wanted to talk to you about something. Gabriela and I have been talking the last few weeks about how much we've enjoyed having you in our lives. You bring such a strong male energy to our relationship, and we feel stronger when we're around you. There's something about having you in this apartment. We really miss your energy when you leave. We would like to extend to you an invitation, and we're hoping you can keep an open mind and heart when you hear it."

As Camila spoke, I was convinced that they were preparing to ask me to be a sperm donor for their child. They had discussed with me their desire to have children at some point. Because they had been together for four years, I assumed they had decided to embark on the next phase of their relationship. I was getting nervous because I didn't know how I really felt about being a sperm donor.

As these thoughts and fears were swirling in my head, they both took my hands and asked in unison, "Would you consider being with us?"

I was completely confused. I didn't know what "being with us" meant. I originally thought that they wanted me to be present for the birth of their child, but they didn't say anything about having a baby.

I then said, "I don't know what you're asking. What do you mean 'be with you?'"

They looked at each other and smiled. Then Gabriela said, "Frank, what we're asking you is whether you would consider joining us—to be in a relationship with us."

The hard drive in my head had stalled, and I didn't know how to press restart.

I then mumbled in confusion, "You're talking about the three of us being in a relationship?"

They nodded very calmly, and Camila said, "I wish I could take credit, but it was Gabriela's idea. She really challenged me to stretch the borders of what it means to be in a relationship."

After she spoke, they could both see my confusion and invited me to speak.

"The thing is, I thought you were lesbians. I didn't know that you were attracted to guys."

Camila slapped me on the knee and said, "Mr. Frank DeVito, you're in danger of failing this course. After so many discussions about the complexity of sexuality, you're asking us this question?" They both began to laugh.

"It's just...I didn't think you saw me in that way. I mean, you're beautiful women, and we've been friends for the past few years. I see you as a couple, and what I'm trying to wrap my head around is why you would want a third wheel. Don't I become the third wheel?"

They looked at each other with concern, and then Camila said, "We don't want you to do something that you don't want to do. We value our friendship with you. Because we've grown to trust you, we're extending this invitation."

"I know what you're feeling," she continued. "What we're proposing is completely against cultural norms. We're committed to living authentic lives, and this feels right for us. If it doesn't feel right for you, we understand."

Camila and Gabriela looked at me intently. They looked so beautiful sitting together. A part of me was afraid of ruining this image I had of them. They were perfect.

To break the tension, I asked, "So, are you asking me to become a Mormon?" They rolled back on the couch, laughing.

To my amazement, I heard the following words come out of my mouth: "I believe in the trinity, the power of three. I'm in. Let's do this."

They began to clap, and they sat next to me as they hugged and kissed me. After we finished our wine, the pita bread, and the hummus, they invited me into their bedroom.

When I woke up the next morning, I was lying at the edge of their queen-size bed. Camila was sleeping in the middle of the bed to my right. She was sleeping on her stomach with her right arm across my chest. Her hair smelled like orange blossoms and coconut. Gabriela was on the other side of the bed. I couldn't see her face because it was covered in a shroud of black hair. I carefully got up and noticed the sun was shining brightly through the windows. It was late Sunday morning—almost noon.

I deliberated whether I should get lunch for us. A thought suddenly pushed itself to the forefront of mind—maybe this was just an experience for them, an experiment. Maybe I didn't understand them; they couldn't possibly have meant for the three of us to be in a relationship. Maybe they just wanted to bond over the experience of doing a threesome. I quietly got dressed and left.

As I drove along Storrow Drive, glancing over at the Charles River and seeing the greenery of the trees and grass flash by me, I thought about my evening with Camila and Gabriela. It didn't seem real, and I was wondering whether I had dreamt the whole episode.

I was also astounded that our lovemaking seemed so easy—it felt like salsa dancing. There was a clear flow and rhythm that I wasn't expecting to experience. When I was in high school, my classmates were constantly sharing their fantasies about being with two women. I never had that dream because one woman seemed overwhelming to me, let alone two.

Around 4:00 p.m., as I was smoking a cigar on my porch, I received a phone call and it was Camila. I could hear the anxiety in her voice as she asked, "Where are you? Why did you leave? Is everything ok?"

I assured her that I was fine, and I apologized for leaving.

"My god, it's ok. It's just that when you left, some triggers went off," explained Camila.

"What do you mean triggers?" I asked.

Camila went on to explain that she and Gabriela had been in long-term relationships with men in Puerto Rico before they became a couple. Both of their significant others had abruptly broken off the relationships. I thought it was ironic that both of them dated men with the same name—Francisco. They were now seeing me, and I shared the same name as their exes.

June 2003 / San Juan, Puerto Rico

As we entered the ornate function room in San Juan, Puerto Rico, Camila introduced me to her father, Don Alejandro Ramirez, and her mother, Doña Valeria Ramirez. They were a stately couple, and I wanted to be them when I grew up.

I extended my hand to Don Alejandro, and he pulled me close for a hug.

He whispered into my ear, "My son, thank you for saving my daughter. I knew she wasn't a lesbian. She just needed a real man to show her that this was just a phase."

Camila frowned because she had heard her father, and then she directed me to a wedding reception line. Her nanny, who had taken care of her when she was growing up, had just married. She was an integral member of Camila's family. After a night of extravagant eating and drinking, Camila drove me to a cabana on the beach where we were staying.

I felt like I was living a dream. I could hear the ocean waves as I made love to Camila. Late at night, we walked along the beach, and I stared up at the stars. Camila leaned into me as we walked, and I intermittently kissed her. When we returned to the cabana, I ordered champagne, and we laughed as we made fun of the wedding guests. Around 5:00 a.m., we heard a soft knock on our door. It was Gabriela.

After I opened the door, Gabriela looked at me sternly with her piercing blue eyes. She then entered the bedroom where Camila had scrambled to put on a robe.

Gabriela then said, "I'm so disappointed with the two of you. I thought our relationship was based on trust and truth. Both of you have lied to me."

Gabriela didn't know that I had accompanied Camila to the wedding. Camila had told her that she was planning on attending alone. Gabriela made the trip to Puerto Rico when she suspected that we had arranged to be together without her.

The three of us had lived in an idyllic trinitarian relationship for three months after our first encounter. My experience in Eden had started coming to an end when I realized that I loved Camila more than Gabriela. Camila had come to the same realization. Gabriela was on the outside looking in, and both of us wondered whether she knew.

On some level, she had to know.

I replied, "I'm sorry, Gabriela. I'm not trying to justify what I've done. I know that I betrayed you. It's just, I didn't know what to expect when we agreed to be together. The past few months have been the happiest days of my life. What happened just happened. This is all new for me. I didn't know where this path would lead me."

Gabriela countered, "That's not an excuse. This is new for me too, but at least I was committed to being honest. What hurts me the most is that the two of you were hiding this from me. Why didn't the two of you say anything?"

Camila then broke into tears saying, "That's a cop-out, Gabriela. You knew and saw what was happening. Yes, I am deeply sorry for the deception, but you also had the moral obligation to say something. Couldn't you see it?"

"Moral obligation? I'm not the one who engaged in an intentional deception. You're throwing that on me? I want the two of you to take responsibility for what you did. You broke my heart, and now you're saying it's my fault," Gabriela said through her tears.

Camila gently replied, "Gabriela, Gabriela, Gabriela, I am taking responsibility. I take total and complete responsibility for my deception and betrayal. I'm just asking you to own your part. You are a victim, but you are a knowing victim. You saw what was happening and you said nothing."

We sat in silence. We cried in silence. There was nothing else to say.

August 2003 / Boston, Massachusetts

Camila and Gabriela were preparing to move to New York City. This had been their original plan. Gabriela and Camila would complete their clinical internships at New York University.

I hadn't spoken to them for over a month since the wedding in San Juan. I made the decision not to see either of them, and had hoped that they could come to some resolution. My real hope was that Camila would leave Gabriela to be with me.

About a week before they left for New York City, I visited them in their apartment to say goodbye. We missed being with each other. They both gave me a long hug. I was hoping to speak to Camila alone, but we didn't have the opportunity. We hadn't really spoken over the phone because both of us felt that she needed to work out what she wanted to do.

The day they left was the day before my birthday, and Camila called to wish me a happy birthday and to say goodbye.

When I asked her what she was planning to do, she said, "Frank, I love you. You're my soul mate. I know this. It's just that I need the year to work out my relationship with Gabriela. I still love Gabriela, and I hurt her very deeply. I need to repair my relationship with her. I don't know what this means, and I can't promise you anything." She continued, "All I can ask for is time. I'm asking you for time. And I'm hoping that you will give me this sacred space. Believe me. I want to be with you. It's just that I need to work through this before I make any decisions. I hope you understand. I hope you can find a way to still love me."

When we finished the phone call, I went to my porch to smoke a cigar. Cigar smoking has always been a meditative practice that allows me to process my thoughts and feelings. As I blew clouds of smoke in the air, I wondered what to do next.

I wanted to wait for Camila, but this felt eerily like my relationship with Sophie. I had waited for a year in anticipation, only to have my hopes crushed. I wasn't sure whether my relationship with Camila was real or an illusion. I didn't want to relive the disappointment I had experienced with Sophie.

I appreciated Camila's honesty. On some level, I understood her dilemma—she loved two people, and she didn't want either of them to be hurt. On another level, I found her request to wait to be a bit selfish.

I knew about the need for space. I had made a similar request of Sophie as I wrestled with my decision about whether or not to be a priest. There was a marked difference: I had been a complete novice. I had had virtually no experience with love relationships. I had only known two women in my life—the priesthood and Sophie. Camila wasn't a novice. She had been in significant relationships with both men and women.

I did want to honor Camila's request to love her the way she wanted to be loved. I had kept my distance from her after our San Juan debacle. I also loved Gabriela. I had exited our fragile trinity because of my role in hurting her.

And finally, I was committed to loving myself. I wanted to embrace the "middle way" between being fully divine and fully human. As Camila once told me, I knew that the only path to an authentic life was from and through the heart. I realized that the key to living an authentic life was to make a choice that honored my heart. This was the central truth of the priesthood that I was still discovering.

I decided not to wait for Camila. Like a snake, I decided to shed skin and remove the parasites of fear that were lodged in my heart. I decided to bet on life and myself. And I was determined to keep playing my hand.

Love would knock on my door again. The mother of my children was patiently waiting on the other side.

CLOSING PRAYER

I am often asked why I left the seminary. Sharing my story about Sophie was the easy and most accessible answer. People often speculated that I had grown frustrated or disillusioned with the institutional Church. This was not the reason. I was rarely successful in confronting this lazy lie. I knew about the Church's well-documented transgressions from an early age. This was never the issue for me because I was always able to distinguish the institutional Church from Catholic spirituality. They are linked but fundamentally different.

The truth is more complex and not as accessible—even to me. I felt deep down that the priest and artist in me could not find expression in the priesthood as defined by the Vatican. I was being called to a love beyond the Vatican.

This love could not be restrained by dogmas, and it extended beyond the walls of churches. It was a love rooted in Jesus' challenge to be perfect (Matthew 5:48), not in the way that the world defines perfection in terms of either winning or losing, succeeding or failing.

Jesus' call to perfection was an invitation to a new priesthood, a priesthood that was a full and complete embrace of the human and the divine, the Hulk and Bruce Banner. Jesus knew that being fully divine and fully human would be a daily grind.

When he taught that we needed to carry our cross daily (Luke 9:23), he wasn't referring to a masochistic approach to life. This misconception is the dominant narrative in too many Christian churches. Jesus was referring to the daily struggle of being a priest and an artist in a world that coerces us to conform and to compromise, to exclude and to demonize, to ignore others' suffering and to scapegoat their pain. Love's perfection is a life without compromise, without playing a role, without being an actor on a stage. It's a life of radical compassion and unfettered passion.

I discovered that being a priest and an artist would be a lonely path. I knew that it was the only path to finding heaven in a world that was fiercely committed to creating hell.

My love relationships reflected this struggle. When I made the decision not to wait for Camila, I was hearing the call for my soul to expand. I initially resisted this calling because I had a deep fear of not finding love again. This is a very common and human experience.

A central tenet of Christianity is the sacred cycle of life and death. This cycle is operative within love—our relationships may end, but love never dies.

Shortly after my breakup with Camila, I met the mother of my children—Danielle Queiroz. She is from Brazil and was a recent immigrant to the United States.

Danielle is a psychologist, and I admired her courage and determination to begin again. She worked as a waitress as she navigated her new life in a new country. Danielle was the first woman—besides my mother—with whom I experienced unconditional love.

My life with Danielle and our children is a story for another book. My hope is that this memoir inspires you to reflect upon the rosary mysteries of your own life and to live a life that is fully human and fully divine.

RESPONSE TO READERS' QUESTIONS

A pilot group of diverse readers read drafts of my memoir, and they posed a number of great questions. In most cases, I did my best to address their questions within the body of the book, but I decided to address some of their questions more explicitly.

Question 1: What was your process for writing the book? Did you start with a plan?

As I stated in the Introduction, I first started by sharing my stories orally as a way to entertain family and friends. After the traumatic premature birth of my children and the death of my daughter, Raquel, in 2008, I was just trying to make sense of my life, and I began drafting stories.

After reading an interview with film director M. Night Shyamalan, I developed a deeper understanding of what I was trying to accomplish. At the turn of the century, he was a celebrated Hollywood director because of his success in the late 1990s and early 2000s, with movies such as *Signs* and *The Sixth Sense*. By the mid-2000s, he had produced a series of flops that lost millions, and he had completely lost his self-confidence, believing that his early success was just luck.

He came home one night after another disastrous box office report on his latest film. He noticed that his wife and daughters were working on a puzzle, and he joined them. As he studied the puzzle pieces, he had an epiphany. He didn't know what the "picture of his life" looked like, but he had to trust that a picture existed while he was working to piece together his life.

I had a similar experience as I was working on my memoir. In my case, I used a metaphorical slide projector, as I explained in the Introduction, to look at key scenes of my life. As I studied these scenes, I realized that there were strong parallels to the mysteries of the rosary. I created a book outline where I aligned key scenes in my life to rosary mysteries. This formed the architecture of my book.

As I began to write, I was in the building phase of constructing the memoir. I wasn't sure how constructing the stories would turn out, but I had three guiding principles: first, I was going to be vulnerable and not focus upon the likability of my character. Second, I wanted to write a memoir that was different from conventional memoirs that followed the Hollywood formula of clear resolutions throughout and at the end of the narrative. This is not life—it's simply how we like to tell stories about life. And third, I wanted to push myself as an artist and find a storytelling style that helped people to get beneath the surface of things. This is why I chose interweaving rather than linear stories.

About midpoint through writing the book, I began to see the arc of the memoir. My story paralleled the story of the protagonist in Hermann Hesse's novel *Siddhartha*. Siddhartha (not the historical Buddha) started as a spiritual seeker who lived an ascetic life as he began his journey and then shifted to a sensual path. He then found a "middle way" which was the source of his personal enlightenment. I saw this arc emerging in my memoir.

Question 2: What did you hope to achieve with this memoir? Did you have an end in mind?

One of the pilot readers best summarized my unstated goals for writing the book with this feedback after reading the initial draft: "I found it so sexy, provocative, and profound."

To be honest, my goals were evolving as I wrote, but her feedback helped me to coalesce my writing around these three goals.

Goal 1: Make it sexy

The world itself is so incredibly sexy. It's full of exquisite sights, scents, and sounds. I wanted to open a door to a sensual experience through my writing. I sprinkled movie and actor analogies throughout the memoir as a tip of the hat to the art of filmmaking in providing powerful sensory experiences. Like a film or good book, I wrote in a way that you could be there with me as I was experiencing everything.

I also find playfulness to be sexy. My writing style is playful. I enjoy seeing the comical in just about everything, and I write as if I were creating a storyboard for Charlie Chaplin.

I find the characters in my life to be sexy. I wanted to communicate how stunning Francesca looked in her red dress, the ethereal eyes of Sophie, and the American apple pie that was Jessica.

Locations are sexy. I wanted you to fall in love with Rome, Salamanca, Cambridge, and even the suburbs of Boston.

And food is so sexy. I wanted you to taste the savoriness of carbonara and feel the heat of a jambalaya.

Goal 2: Make it provocative

I believe that the soil—yes, the soil—of something truly provocative is vulnerability. Without vulnerability, something can be shocking, but it will lack authenticity and emotional depth. This is why I had to let go of likability when I wrote my memoir. I wanted to expand our understanding of what it means to be the hero of our lives. We've been hypnotized by Hollywood and the popular media to see the world as comprising simply heroes and villains. This is the great lie.

For example, I found myself annoyed when I saw the very emotional tributes to basketball All-Star Kobe Bryant. I thought it was due to jealousy or the fact that I was a Boston Celtics fan. I then read an article by ESPN commentator, Ramona Shelburne, where she reminded us that Kobe wasn't perfect: he was accused of rape in 2003 and had reached a settlement with the victim. Shelburne was barraged by angry fans and fellow media commentators who accused her of defaming Kobe's name. As a collective culture, we could not embrace Kobe in all of his complexity. He had to be framed as a hero or a villain. I didn't want my memoir to fall into the trap where I presented myself as the likable hero with a perfect happy ending. The truth is that like Kobe, I am a deeply flawed hero and recovering villain working towards an ambiguous but hopeful ending.

Some readers were stunned when a luminous mystery opened with a graphic sex scene with Jennifer, a student teacher. My intent was not to shock but to highlight a transition in my memoir as I was entering the sensual path of my life. The description of the scene was not crude; it was sensual and playful. How something is described says more than what is described.

We don't usually juxtapose sex with the rosary—unless you're the singer Madonna. I wanted to challenge the reader to reconsider the role of sexuality in the development of our personal identity and the way we understand the world.

In the West, we tend to divorce sexuality from the religious, the spiritual, the ethical, and the moral. Sex has no place in the rosary. I don't believe that God or the universe operates this way. The universe is an orgasm of beauty, wonder, awe, and mystery. It is fundamentally physical, and without the physical, we can never find the spiritual.

I believe the most provocative quote of all time comes from Jesuit priest, philosopher, and paleontologist Pierre Teilhard de Chardin. He wrote, "We are not human beings having a spiritual experience. We are spiritual beings having a human experience."

In the West, we have it upside down: we believe that the spiritual resides in the abstract, the absolute, and the immutable. The reality is that our path to truth and love begins in the soil—the granular, the mossy, and the rocky. We can only enter the divine through the human. This is Jesus. This is the central mystery of the incarnation.

Goal 3: Make it profound

This was the trickier aspect of the memoir. I am a junkie when it comes to philosophy, theology, the social sciences, and the physical sciences.

However, I knew that this was not the case for many potential readers as I drafted the memoir. The Vatican and the priesthood might stir some interest with readers. Some might connect with my experiences as a teacher. And others would be engaged with the love stories. But I wanted to go deeper.

I had an epiphany as I was reading a book by one of my favorite spiritual writers. As I read chapter after chapter, I was impressed with his profound insight, but a problem emerged when he provided personal experiences to illustrate his insight. The anecdotes came across as tinny.

I then realized that the challenge was that he started with an abstract insight, and then he tried to give it flesh and bones. His attempt to incarnate his ideas, in my opinion, wasn't successful because his focus wasn't the story but the abstract principles that they illustrated. In other words, the stories were secondary or even tertiary.

As humans, we are wired to understand reality through the medium of stories. A story is like giving someone the experience of smelling and touching a rose. An abstract spiritual reflection is like offering someone a rose by giving a petal, and then another petal, and then a thorn, and then a piece of a stem. The person never has the full experience of holding and smelling a rose. I led with stories, and I told them in a way that readers were invited to consider their meaning. This is why Jesus used parables—he knew that they served as wormholes to deeper spiritual and human insights.

My hope is that this memoir inspires you to delve into your own stories and to find mediums through which to express them. They don't have to be written as memoir; they could be expressed through journaling, poetry, drama, the visual arts, music, and/or movement— whatever inspires you. I also hope that as you engage in this process, you will connect more closely to your authentic self. This may upset other people because you're not conforming to their expectations. Fuck them. God and the universe will be cheering you on.

Question 3: Your memoir covers a range of love stories with very different women in usual and unusual contexts. What have you learned about the nature of love and relationships?

When I began drafting a response to this question, my son Francesco, who was eleven at the time, ran up to me and said, "*Papai*, I'm in love with Joey. I need your help because I'm afraid she's getting bored with me."

Joey is a beautiful Dominican girl who lives in our neighborhood. They were inseparable, but because of COVID-19, they had to rely upon texting to communicate. I thought his request for help was cute, and I had this conversation with him:

"Well first of all, you're a beautiful kid. She's not going to get bored with you. Why do you think she's bored?" I asked.

"Papai, when I text her, she doesn't seem too excited to text back. I'm afraid I'm going to lose her. I love her too much to lose her."

I wanted to tell him to join the club, but I didn't want to snuff out the flames of young love. I asked Francesco for his phone and read through the texts.

I then said to him, "Francesco, you use a lot of emojis to say that you love her, but you don't say why you love her. You've also sent her a hundred texts about the games that you play online together. She may not want to spend all her time talking about that."

"Then what should I talk to Joey about? You gotta help me, Papai," pleaded Francesco.

I was laughing to myself at the thought of coaching my son about love when he was only eleven, but I took on the challenge.

"OK—here's the thing. Girls need to know that you notice things about them that are special. What do you love about Joey?" I asked.

"I love her hair. She has beautiful hair," Francesco enthusiastically replied.

"That's great, but I want you to describe what you love about her hair. Girls want to know that you notice the small things that other people may not see," I advised.

"Well, she keeps her hair in a bun, but when she lets it down, it has this zigzag flow that I love," he replied.

"Francesco! We are in business! You love the zigzag flow of her hair. I love that. OK, how do you feel when you see her hair?" I asked.

He thought about it for a few seconds and said, "Her zigzag hair makes me happy when I'm sad."

I kissed him on the forehead and said, "Oh my God, that's so beautiful. Type that to her right now."

"Papai! She just texted me a hundred heart emojis! What should I send next?" Francesco asked, jumping off the sofa.

"Here's the thing: a girl wants to know that you love what's inside of her and not just the outside. What's something very sweet that you love about Joey?"

"Well, when we're playing, she always has my back. When someone is trying to kill me, she tries to protect me," he replied.

I was less than enthusiastic to find out that he played a lot of *Fortnite* with Joey, but I let it go. "OK, she protects you. That's a beautiful thing. Tell her how much you appreciate that she protects you."

Francesco did a flip on the couch when Joey sent another flurry of heart emojis.

"Papai, you're really good at this. How come you don't have a girlfriend?"

Ouch. Francesco reminded me that I was good at giving advice about love as long as I didn't have to engage in it. The women in my life were my teachers, and I was a very difficult student. These were the lessons I learned.

Lesson 1: True love requires a fierce commitment to vulnerability.

Unfortunately, I have a relentless tendency not to be vulnerable. In the Glorious Mysteries, I stated that I was "love's angel of death." What I meant was that I was always going to break a woman's heart because I could not get beyond the ideal of love as a perfect marble statue of Aphrodite. The problem is that even statues have cracks, and when the cracks began to be apparent both in myself and in my partner, my first instinct was either to isolate myself within the relationship or to bolt.

I also learned that true love requires us to be vulnerable to the sacred ending of a relationship. It doesn't mean that love dies—love is transformed. When I'm at a wedding and hear the words "until death do us part," I say a prayer for the couple that they understand that death's parting does not necessarily mean a physical death. True love requires that we are vulnerable to sacred endings. An ending is sacred when we embrace our own feelings of pain as our relationships go through transitions. An ending is sacred when we allow ourselves to experience not-being-in-control. Surrendering to what we cannot control is the most powerful stance of vulnerability.

Our culture focuses upon the transactional nature of relationships—you're either winning or losing. As long as life is framed as winning or losing, authenticity is often lost. People don't want their relationship to "fail." We love that elderly couple who celebrates their seventy-fifth wedding anniversary, and we ask them what the key was to their "success" in marriage. In my mind, they are together because they chose to stay together. It could have been a good choice, or it could have been a tragic choice. We don't know. Just like we don't know how long a person will live and why someone lives long or dies young.

Lesson 2: True love requires honesty even if it's going to hurt like hell.

In the case of Hilary, and Camila and Gabriela, I intentionally deceived them because I did not want to deal with the fallout of telling them the truth. Lying or deception is always a bad idea—that's why it's one of the Ten Commandments.

Lesson 3: True love means subverting our culture's addiction to romantic love.

I called romantic love "the greatest lie ever told" in the Glorious Mysteries. I believe that every relationship requires a commitment to romance, but romantic love poses the temptation to not be our authentic selves. I defined Jessica as the "wrong kind of person to love" (a.k.a. the whore) because of her open sensuality and playfulness. I chose to be with Hilary for three years because she was the safe choice—I could check off all the boxes for what it meant to be in a "successful relationship." In the case of Angelina, she was the trophy girlfriend/wife who was going to pay dividends in the social stock market.

That said, I don't want people mistreating their lovers with a paucity of romance because they don't want to engage in the illusion of romantic love. If anything, turn it up, and in some cases, turn it up to eleven.

Lesson 4: True love means blasting through cultural and social norms of how we define relationships.

My relationship with Camila and Gabriela was a very happy one, but I didn't allow myself to completely enjoy it because I could always see the moral police in my rearview mirror. In retrospect, I wonder whether I sabotaged that relationship because I didn't want to deal with the social fallout—to be a pariah.

In the final Luminous Mystery, Camila and Gabriela detailed the amazing diversity of sexual identity and gender. Within our culture, we force fit people into social conventions and then invoke God to justify our biphobia, homophobia, and transphobia. I believe that in the future—and hopefully, the not-too-distant future—we will have diverse and equitable relationship structures that honor our human diversity.

I want to be clear that I believe that celibacy can be a legitimate and authentic choice, too. Choosing to be celibate doesn't mean that something is wrong with you. Again, we live in a culture that is always ready to label people as problems. Just to clarify—being single is not the same as being celibate. Celibacy is a commitment not to engage in sex—this could be for personal or religious reasons. A single person may engage in sex but choose not to be in a partner relationship. Both are legitimate choices that our culture rarely values.

Some people believe that the sexual abuse crisis in the Catholic Church was related to the problem of celibacy—it wasn't. The problem was the culture of the Church in advancing the ultimate transaction—protecting its own rather than the innocent. This happens in business, education, politics, and in any institution: the innocent become collateral damage when the system is only interested in maintaining the power and authority of a few.

I am still a novice in this thing called love. I continue to fail and fall, but I am fiercely committed to dancing. I will continue to dance with love, and step on her toes, and drop her multiple times. But I know that there will be moments when I will be as graceful as Fred Astaire, and she will be proud to be my partner.

Question 4: What is your view of the Catholic Church? What are some of your core or evolving beliefs about religion and spirituality?

One of the most underrated and esoteric parables of Jesus was when he compared the Kingdom of God to laborers working in a vineyard (Matthew 20:1-16). In the parable, a landowner hires laborers early in the morning to work in his vineyard. The landowner then goes out and hires workers at 9:00 a.m., 12:00 p.m., 3:00 p.m., and even as late as 5:00 p.m.

In the evening, the landowner instructs his foreman to pay the laborers, beginning with the ones who started working at 5:00 pm. The laborers who began working early in the morning assumed that they would be paid more, but they protested when they saw that they received the same payment as the laborers who started working at 5:00 p.m. The landowner then tells them that he has every right to pay whatever he wants to pay. The parable then ends with a line that most people know: "The last shall be first, and the first shall be last."

If you hear this parable read in a church, a priest or preacher will most likely go on to give a homily or sermon about the generosity of God.

To my mind, this story is one of the most subversive parables in the gospels, and it provides the most complete vision of what Jesus meant by the "Kingdom of God." Jesus is shining a spotlight on the transactional way that religion operates and the transactional ways that we live our lives. This transactional dynamic not only operates in religion but is the basic operating system in our culture.

Turn on any religious TV station, and you will see a transactional understanding of faith. If you just believe hard enough—or donate enough money—you can achieve prosperity, health, and a successful life. Go into any self-help aisle in a bookstore, and you will see a thousand books about ten ways to be successful in money, marriage, and your career. Life is about winning and losing. If I get more, someone else has to get less. It's the source of xenophobia in this country and around the world.

This was a dangerous and subversive parable, and Jesus was brutally killed for it.

I loved, and still love, Catholic spirituality because, at its core, it advances the vision of Jesus as creating a world that has an operating system of radical compassion for equity. "The last shall be first" is the mantra to remind us that no one should be measured, mistreated, or excluded because of their race, class, religion, beliefs, gender, sexuality, or ethnicity. We measure people every day, and they either satisfy our internal accounting, or they don't. We measure people by their appearance, their net worth, their education, their status, their job, their partners, their kids, and the "they seem to have it all together" appearance of their lives.

We are terrified to step outside this market exchange because we don't know who we are or what we would do. My Catholic heroes left the marketplace: Saint Francis, Óscar Romero, and Dorothy Day. My other heroes who were not Catholic but who shared a common vision were Malcolm X, Martin Luther King Jr., and Cesar Chavez. We've replaced them with billionaires who decide what's good for us and celebrities who expound on how to be successful. And in both cases, they reap the rewards of an unjust system that was designed to serve them.

The whole thing is a lie, and Jesus wanted to burn it all down (Luke 12:49 and Matthew 21:12-13).

So if Jesus is upending a transactional way of living, what is the operating system of the Kingdom of God? I believe that love for Jesus represents the power of compassionate collaboration to go beyond a win or lose framing of reality.

According to Jesus, the key to a loving collaboration was making sure that "the first shall be last." This meant that the focus of any collaboration should be to ensure that the most vulnerable among us are the priority—this is radical compassion or collaboration for equity. This completely flips the current power dynamics in our culture where collaborative efforts, mostly in the form of manipulation, are meant to benefit the wealthy and the powerful. In the case of COVID-19, imagine if our focus had been to protect the most vulnerable? This would have guided all our decisions—not the morass of decision-making where our priorities were never established, and then in the end, banks and big businesses would find a way to benefit from the pain of others. This was the pain of Jesus.

What I find astounding and encouraging is that I know more atheists and agnostics who share this vision of Jesus. They are committed to a more truly collaborative—not transactional—world, and they are working daily to address our deep social inequities.

When it comes to my relationship with the institutional Catholic Church, I still have a deep respect and love for the Church. I shared in the Sorrowful Mysteries how my father taught me the distinction between Catholic spirituality and the institution. He never, however, denigrated the Catholic Church. He just pointed out the reality of its profound dysfunction.

The dysfunction was always related to the transactional way that it operated. This was the basis for the rallying cry of Martin Luther and the Reformation. The Church made the claim to own the priesthood, marriage, love, life, and even death. The claim was always absurd. It was like a child scooping up a pail of water and then making a claim to own the ocean.

I still remain a Catholic because I believe in the power of community. Catholicism, with all its warts, provides a deep community for billions of people around the world. Without Catholicism, there is no Saint Francis or Dorothy Day. Without Catholicism, this book does not exist.

I loved the advice of the Dalai Lama when he was asked whether people should turn to Buddhism. He replied that people should delve into the faith of their families and ancestors. He believed there was a reason why people were born into a particular faith. They should only turn to Buddhism after this journey. In his wisdom, he knew that if people really explored and lived the core tenets of Christianity, Judaism, Islam, or any of the major world religions, they would find their way home.

I believe that finding our way home is deeply rooted in being fully divine and fully human. If you're an atheist, or an agnostic, or you come from a tradition that does not believe in the divine, replace the term *divine* with "being our true and best selves." I used the analogy of Bruce Banner and the Hulk to describe the divine and human, but I caution not to equate Bruce Banner exclusively with the divine and the Hulk with the human. The divine and the human exist in both Bruce Banner and in the Hulk—just as the divine and the human exist both in the priest and the artist. They are not meant to be bifurcated. I was trying to find the language to explain a profound mystery. The mystery cannot be understood; it can only be lived.

Question 5: What are your core or evolving beliefs about education?

I have a confession. When we went into a worldwide quarantine because of COVID-19, I welcomed it. I wanted everything to stop, and I especially wanted schools to stop. While I welcomed it, I was also aware of the devastating effects it was having on the working poor and communities of color. They didn't have the luxury of just staying at home and watching Netflix.

I welcomed the COVID-19 shutdown because I believe that public education is more dysfunctional than the Catholic Church could or would ever be. Our public schools are factories for transactional living. We tell kids that they need to learn something for a test, or to get into a great college, or to land a high-paying job. Learning is a transaction, and if you are a student, teacher, or parent who doesn't want any part of it, you are punished by the system.

Since 2012, I've been working with a team to develop an education model that we hope spreads like a virus—in a good way— throughout the world. Our model is called Equity Lab, and we are working to advance the following core values:

Creativity. Creativity is the act of conceptualizing new and imaginative ideas that lead to novel applications and solutions. Creativity is characterized by the ability to perceive the world in new ways, to find hidden patterns, to make connections between seemingly unrelated phenomena, and to generate solutions. According to cognitive science, creativity is one of the highest cognitive skills, and researchers have discovered that creative insights are based upon two cognitive operations that are happening at the same time in different parts of the brain. In one operation, called associative or divergent thinking, thoughts are intuitive and explore an expansive range of possibilities. The other operation is convergent thinking, the ability to analyze and synthesize. Both operations need to be engaged for the creative process to emerge.

Innovation. At the intersection of creativity and need is innovation. Innovation is the implementation of a new or significantly improved product, service, or process that creates value for a community sector such as business, education, government, or health and human services. For example, Dr. Maria Montessori noticed that students in Rome—especially those with special needs—struggled with traditional classroom pedagogy. Through innovative thinking, she developed a new approach where students would be allowed to explore their individual pursuits, and in the process, arrive at a much higher level of learning than their peers who were taught in traditional classrooms. Innovation is the powerful application of a creative idea to address a real social problem and the ability to see it through to implementation. Innovation requires developing a deep sense of resilience because as a creative idea becomes a reality, obstacles will be encountered and mistakes will be made.

Collaboration. Aristotle's powerful insight "the whole is greater than the sum of its parts" is the core meaning of collaboration. The late Steve Jobs stated in a number of interviews that Apple products were possible only because his team believed in the power of collaboration. Cognitive research supports this approach: new solutions, models, and innovative ways of thinking usually happen among peer groups discussing and wrestling with problems together. Given the increasing complexity of the workplace and our social challenges, the synergy of collaboration will be an essential requirement for students as they navigate the twenty-first century.

Social Responsibility. Social responsibility is the emerging awareness that our actions and decisions have ethical consequences. It's developmentally essential for adolescents to have opportunities to discover their power as change agents in their families, schools, and communities. They try on and experiment with different roles as they interact with peers and adults. Cultivating an ethic of compassion and a sense of responsibility to others is a critical step in their self-discovery. Providing students with opportunities to exercise social responsibility is critical to help them develop a sense of purpose and to discover their unique talents.

So that's the dream. There are schools both within the United States and around the world that are advancing this vision. The problem is that they are oases in a desert of inequity.

The challenge is that our public schools reflect the deeper inequities in our society. The problem is not our teachers: they are heroes trying to put out fires that they are not equipped to handle. The problem is not our students: they are incredibly resilient as they face daily doses of racism, sexism, and classism. The problem is not our parents: they live in a xenophobic world that is rigged against them.

The problem is that the system is resistant to deep change because too many power brokers are benefiting from the inequity of the system. The testing industry does not want anyone to ask why millions of dollars are invested in testing primarily Black and brown children rather than being reinvested to improve the quality of our educational programs. Federal, state, and local bureaucrats rely on testing to provide evidence that they are "winning" in closing the "achievement gap" while everyone knows it is an opportunity gap. It's the difference between winning or losing an election or landing a multimillion dollar contract to provide products and services to schools that they do not need.

I still believe in public education like I believe in the Catholic Church. My hope is that COVID-19 serves as a catalyst for everyone to collectively examine the problems with our educational system. My fear is that we will keep doing the same things and just do it remotely rather than in person.

I am a cautious optimist.

Question 6: Sometimes the connections between your memoir and the rosary are not apparent. How are they connected?

This is a good question. Below I briefly outline the connections. You may still disagree with the connections, but that's the beauty of art and truth—we can always agree to disagree.

JOYFUL MYSTERIES

1. The Annunciation. The angel Gabriel announces to Mary that she will give birth to Jesus. "Gift Box." Just as Mary wrestles with the fear that her life is about to drastically change because she will become the mother of Jesus, I am wrestling with my fear that my life will completely change as I consider leaving the seminary.

2. The Visitation. Mary visits her cousin Elizabeth, who is pregnant with John the Baptist. "Apartment Phone." Just as Mary visits Elizabeth and shares the good news with her, Sophie visits my apartment to invite me to embark on a new phase of my life.

3. The Nativity of Jesus, or Jesus' birth. "99 Red Balloons." Just as shepherds and the magi are traveling to Bethlehem to see Jesus, tourists are converging onto the Duomo, or dome of Cathedral of Santa Maria del Fiore in Florence, Italy.

4. The Presentation of the Lord. Mary's presentation of Jesus in the Temple of Jerusalem. "Convent Courtyard." My love for Sophie becomes a public act when the nuns see us kissing in the convent courtyard.

5. Finding Jesus in the Temple of Jerusalem. "Frigid Miracles." Pilgrims such as Diego and Arthur find Jesus through their healings at Our Lady of Lourdes.

SORROWFUL MYSTERIES

1. The Agony of Jesus in the Garden of Gethsemane. "Father Andrew." I experience the agony of losing my father.

2. Jesus is scourged. "Bambino Gesù." The parents of Carla experience their own anguish and scourging in the death of their daughter.

3. Jesus is crowned with thorns. "Candidacy." I experience the public humiliation of announcing my departure from the seminary.

4. Jesus carries the cross. "Shower Curtain." I carry the cross or burden of a traumatic experience.

5. The Crucification of Jesus. "Last Supper." I experience death with the loss of Francesca and Sophie.

GLORIOUS MYSTERIES

1. The Resurrection of Jesus. "Pathways." The door of Chelsea High School, and a new life, is opened to me just as Mary Magdalene discovered the open entrance of the empty tomb.

2. The Ascension of Jesus to Heaven. "California Dreamin'." Jesus commissions the apostles to spread the "good news" just as Pathways is commissioned to live out its educational mission.

3. The Descent of the Holy Spirit. "Prom Dress." The Holy Spirit empowers Jesus' disciples to be agents of love just as Pathways empowers students to be agents of change.

4. The Assumption of Mary into Heaven. "Couples Therapy." Mary is brought to heaven body and soul just as I let go of Hilary who is my personal image of Mary.

5. Mary is Crowned as Queen of Heaven and Earth. "234 Lakeview." Just as Mary is crowned queen of heaven and earth, Milena becomes the woman and queen of my life.

LUMINOUS MYSTERIES

1. The Baptism of Jesus in the Jordan River. "Coffee Shop Confession." Just as Jesus is anointed by John the Baptist to begin his public ministry, I receive a personal anointing to hear the confession of the Colombian man.

2. The Wedding at Cana. "Want Ad." Jesus changes water into wine at a wedding, and I experienced the inverse in a failed wedding proposal.

3. Jesus Spreads the "Good News" of the Kingdom of God. "New York Minute." At a retreat in New Hampshire, I share my understanding of Jesus' vision with Jack, and at a middle school in New York City, I help them to create a new school vision.

4. The Transfiguration. "Carnaval in the Subway." Jesus is transfigured in divine light, revealing who he really is, just as the vision of teens dancing samba in the subway gives me a vision of the heart of life.

5. The Last Supper. "Fragile Trinity." Jesus uses a meal to redefine what it means to be in a true community just as Camila and Gabriela reveal to me what it means to be in an authentic relationship or community.

Question 7: I know this book is a memoir, but I was wondering if everything you wrote about was actually true. Some of the stories have the choreography of a movie. And how did you remember and write all that dialogue?

All the events I wrote about are completely true—as I remembered them. And that's key because we know from cognitive science that our memory can play tricks on us. Any true story is a unique presentation of a person's reality, and I presented you my version. When I shared my stories with families and friends, I found it helpful to hear their versions. Listening to their versions did influence how I remembered the stories. Memory can be a collective exercise, and that's valuable because then a story has more complexity and depth.

You may have noticed a glitch in the memoir's chronology when I shared the story of Hilary. In the therapist's office, I stated that I had been with Hilary for three years. If you were paying attention, I was actually with her for two years. What had occurred is that Hilary's sister, in an earlier scene at the beach, said to my date that Hilary and

I had been together for three years. I accepted this assertion without question, and it became my reality. It was not until my editors caught this discrepancy that I realized how powerfully another person's assertion can influence our own understanding of reality.

I believe that a great book or movie has a beautiful and unique choreography. The story can be powerful, but poor craft or execution will always submarine the story. The reverse is also true—great craft cannot overcome a crappy story.

I did my best to write the stories using choreography, so you could dance with them and feel that you're in the story with me. As far as the dialogue, cognitive science has revealed that memory is related to meaning—the significance of a particular event—and the level of emotions connected to that event. The stories and characters I'm sharing with you have deep ruts in my mind and heart. If I have a high emotional connection to an event, I can remember what people were wearing and how they smelled, what we ate and how it tasted and smelled.

It was the same with the conversations that I had with people. I don't pretend that the conversations in this memoir are meeting minutes, but they do accurately reflect the content. I was able to reconstruct dialogue because I not only remembered what was said but how it was said. I wanted you to experience the choreography of how people spoke which is why I included Italian, French, and Spanish in some of the dialogue. For example, Francesca had a beautiful cadence when she spoke in Italian, and there was an elegant stiltedness when she spoke in English. Likewise, Camila and Gabriela both spoke English with a stiltedness that I found musical. Jack Donovan is a Jersey Joe, and he has always spoken like one. I have vivid memories about how the people in my life spoke and what they cared about. I tried my best to honor that in the dialogue.

Question 8: In the introduction you mentioned that you began writing as a therapeutic exercise to deal with the traumatic birth of your children and the loss of your daughter, Raquel. Why did your memoir begin in the years before this personal tragedy? Are you planning on writing future books?

I did begin writing about the birth of my children and the death of my daughter, Raquel, shortly after these events occurred. They were stories within my personal journal. The challenge was that these stories were deeply personal, and I hadn't really shared them with family and friends. As I stated in my introduction, I think deeply personal stories need to ferment in our hearts before we share them. The heart understands things before our mind grasps them; the journey needs to go from the heart to the head. This takes time and some emotional distance.

I also believe that stories need a piloting phase where they are shared in intimate and informal settings. I had done this with my stories about the seminary and my teaching days in Chelsea. My friend Sergio, the Brazilian actor featured in the Luminous Mysteries, did not believe that Marlon Brando was a great actor. We agreed to disagree. I believe Brando was a great actor because he knew the value of playing with lines before the final cut. That's why he loved to do multiple takes. He wanted to see how certain lines sounded in a scene and also see the reaction of his fellow actors as he played with his lines. His acting and character development was an iterative and collaborative process. I was ready to write this memoir because I had been through a similar process.

My hope and my goal is to write future memoirs. I may even have a few novels up my sleeve. I just love telling stories.

CPSIA information can be obtained
at www.ICGtesting.com
Printed in the USA
BVHW071350141221
624009BV00009B/814